1

First Published in Great Britain:

2021

Loch Ness Book Publishing

lochnessbooks@btinternet.com

Copyright © Sinclair Gair

Published by: Loch Ness Book Publishing, lochnessbooks@btinternet.com

Books in the series:
Alexander Battan Grant – His Legacy
Alexander Battan Grant – Fisherman, Musician & Fiddler of Note
Two Highland Fiddlers + 2
The Scottish Highlands Fiddle and Piping Heritage
Pipe Major William Collie Ross

ISBN: 978-1-8383993-1-3

Acknowledgements:

The inspiration and guidance to start this project came about from one of my many visits to Donald Fraser's Ironmongers shop in Beauly. This shop was sometime previously owned by Donald Morison (associate of Grant and first assistant leader of the Highland Strathspey and Reel Society), and as it turned out, has been the repository over many years of interesting exhibits relating to Alexander Grant i.e. one of his violins in beautiful playable condition, James Scott Skinner's actual Will and large framed photographic print, plus many other items of note. I was shown all of this collection in an up-stairs wood panelled (old fashioned style) room which would fit the description of 'time capsule' very accurately.

This was in November 2017 and I had never heard the name Battan Grant mentioned anywhere. In discussion with Donald he further revealed the extent to which Grant had gained fame in his fishing achievements and patented fishing rod design. It seemed to Donald that Grant had been wronged by others at a later time when they claimed to have broken his distance fly casting British championship record - when in fact they had not used the same method of casting.

Donald summed it all up by saying "the man should be better known among the general public for his outstanding achievements across a wide range of activities and interests".

A few days later Donald provided me with historical written accounts of Grants life. On reading these I found myself in complete agreement with his sentiments and this undertaking was started from there.

The work progressed to having several meetings with the Curator of Inverness Museum and Art Gallery, Kari Moodie, who very supportively gave me access to the Museum's records on Grant. In particular, access to the contents of Grant's workshop held in the store room, which were bequeathed to the Museum. Some of these are on display in the viewing area together with exhibits relating to his pupil and associate Donald Riddell.

A particular acknowledgement is due to Michael Kerr, great grandson of Alexander Grant. Michael has, for the greater part of his life, had a keen interest in Grant, and has researched his background and family history in great detail. The author is truly grateful to have been given access to this scholarly piece of research.

In completion of the work, I wish to extend my thanks for the support received from todays top Highland fiddlers by their inputs, particularly Duncan Chisholm, and Bruce MacGregor, thereby enabling me to accurately record the cultural legacy and heritage Section to date. They represent the very top level of achievement traceable through Donald Riddell back to Grant, and from which the future development of this unique musical tradition will be traced.

Finally, I am very grateful to have been able to use the excellent facilities provided by the Highland Archive Service in Inverness – particularly ambaile.org.uk . A clear indication that we are an educated and cultured race of people in Scotland.

Authors Note:

Part 1 of this book compilation have been re-produced largely from documents held in the files of Inverness Museum and Art Gallery (IMAG), Inverness – most of which are (at this time) available to view online (at www.ambaile.org.uk), and historical records held by Donald Fraser at Morisons Ironmongers, Beauly. Michael Kerr, Grant's great grandson, has contributed his considerable family history research material and family archive photographs. All in all, these form an important and accurate account of Grant's life and will give future readers a valuable insight of Grant's life and times. Duncan Chisholm, and Bruce MacGregor have both contributed testimonials in appreciation of their teacher, Donald Riddell. Donald was a pipe major in the Lovat Scouts, was taught to play the violin by Grant, and also how to make violins. The teaching tradition of both these gentlemen are now being passed onto a future generation.

It has not been the intention to "tell a story" about Alexander Grant. The specific purpose has been to collect all of the known written factual accounts of his life and activities, and to trace his heritage through to the current day. Elsewhere I have used short narratives to enhance the flow and link sections together.

There is a voluminous record of correspondence which Grant received from James Scot Skinner which Grant meticulously kept. (Available in the book 'Alexander Battan Grant – his life and legacy', by the author, and available in Inverness Museum reference section). The information contained in the book provides a very valuable archive on Skinner.

FOREWARD BY LORD LOVAT

To quote Alexander 'Battan' Grant – An imperfect job is no use to anyone which is not the case with Sinclair Gair's scholarly story of Two Highland Fiddlers.

I knew very little about either of these 2 gentlemen but was well acquainted with the portrait of my uncle Hugh sitting holding his fiddle made by Donald Riddell. Having read and enjoyed Sinclair Gair's book I cannot recommend it more highly to musicians, historians and people with a love of the Highlands.

Simon Lovat

16th Lord Lovat, 5th Baron, and 24th Chief of the Clan Fraser

Lovat Estate Office,

Beauly,

Inverness-shire,

Scotland.

May 2021

His motto:

"Either a thing is right or it isn't, and if it isn't, it's not worth troubling about". Similarly, "Why" he said, "take any trouble at all unless you are going to take enough? An imperfect job is no use to anyone".

Alexander 'Battan' Grant

1856 – 1942

(His Life and Legacy)

CONTENTS

Alexander 'Battan' Grant

1856 – 1942

(His Life and Legacy)

(Photograph of an Alexander Grant fiddle, owned by Donald Fraser at Donald

Morisons, Ironmonger, Beauly – courtesy Laura Fraser)

Part 1

INTRODUCTION – an overview of his achievements

Alexander Grant

(Studio Portrait)

Alexander 'Battan' Grant

Alexander Battan Grant

(With his cap back to front as always)

Highland Fiddle Maker and Champion Fisherman

Alexander Grant was born in Battangorm, on Spey-side, in 1856 and played a vital role in keeping alive in the Highlands the tradition of Strathspey playing as it had developed during the 18th century. Popularly known as "Battan", because of his birth-place (Battangorm Croft, near Carrbridge), he was a close friend of James Scott Skinner (1843 – 1927), the brilliant and colourful composer and exponent of Strathspey playing. Grant died in Inverness in 1942.

It is said that Grant took his first violin lesson at the age of ten, but refused to go back because the tone of the teacher's violin was so bad. Even allowing for some exaggeration, this story accurately reflects Grant's interest in the sound quality of the instrument – a subject which preoccupied him for most of his life. He probably made his first fiddles while still in his early twenties, although the earliest Grant fiddle known at the present time dates from 1886, when the maker was already thirty.

Making a fiddle

Throughout his life, Grant was never satisfied simply with copying the violin designs of Italian masters such as Stradivari or Guarneri and there are numerous examples of his experimenting with different designs. A beautifully finished guitar-shaped instrument is in the Museum's collections, dated 1892 and probably based on a design of Stradivari dating from c.1726. The tone of the instrument, however, cannot compare with its looks. It is marked "No.1 Battangorm" and no other example of this design is known, indicating perhaps that Grant was dissatisfied with the resulting tone.

There are a number of significant departures particularly in the materials used by Grant to make his fiddles which reflect both his personality and local conditions. Normally, maple wood is used for the fiddle back, sides and neck, and pine or spruce for the front, but many of Grant's fiddles have bog-fir fronts – a wood which because of its immense age, possess better sound characteristics, but is harder to obtain. The fiddles made from this material have a particularly fine tone. Another violin in the Museum's collections bears the label, in Grant's handwriting: "Strad make – late 1600. Front restored and whole body re-balanced giving correct relationship, by Alex. Grant (Battan), Inverness 1900". Whether or not the instrument is a genuine Stradivari, clearly Grant believed it was, and was confident enough of his own ability to feel he could improve on the original by filling the f-holes slightly, and thinning down the front and back. The instrument as it is now certainly sounds superb.

The sound quality of any violin depends on a large number of complex and interacting variables, such as the relationship between the front and back, the thickness and type of wood used, the angle of arching, the volume of air inside, and the type and thickness of varnish applied to the finished instrument – among many other factors. Grant's genius lay in so regulating these critical factors that his fiddles were much praised in his own time, and, are still played and valued today.

Each fiddle would have taken him about 150 hours to make, and consisted of either 81 or 82 parts, depending on whether the back was made in two halves, or as a single whole. Grant does not seem to have felt it essential to make all the parts of his instruments himself, as some makers like to do, for most of the pegs and finger boards on his existing fiddles are clearly purchased, and among his tools were found a considerable number of partly-finished, manufactured sides, fronts and backs, which Grant would subsequently have worked down to the desired thicknesses. He must have been an extremely methodical man, for the contents of his workshop which have been acquired by the Museum testify again and again to his neatness and tidiness: even the smallest items such as bridges, and sound posts have been sorted into individual tin boxes, which fit neatly within other boxes for storage. To make the fiddle, he used an inside mould, around which the sides of the fiddle were built up, glued and clamped together. Grant never seems to have had a fiddle-making workshop as such, preferring to work at home in an upstairs room, as he did for the majority of his active life at Tomnahurich farm house, Inverness. This room seems to have been something of a private place, into which even close friends were not allowed, Grant preferring to bring examples of his work, for example, downstairs to be looked at and discussed.

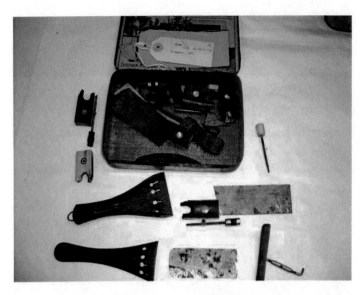

For Grant, fiddle-making was always a spare-time pursuit – although of over-riding importance to him – and never a means of earning a living. This he did in many ways, becoming a ploughman on leaving school, and thereafter shepherd, forester, gamekeeper, fisherman, grocer, hairdresser and fishing tackle merchant, before taking the tenancy of Tomnahurich Farm at the turn of the century. Grant's grandfather had been a woodturner and something of a clock maker, so it is perhaps not surprising that at the age of 18 he went to Cullen to learn forestry. This, however, he had to give up after a short time due to poor health, which plagued him for several years afterwards. However, throughout his life he had a passionate interest in what he called "the rhythmic or vibratory qualities of wood".

The Grant Vibration Rod

This interest resulted in his invention of a unique design of fishing rod, based on principles which are closely allied to those of the fiddle – a rod which is still widely used nearly 80 years later. The rods were in two, three or four sections, usually made of green-heart, each section being joined to the other by overlapping splices, held in place by leather thonging. Because of the constant vibrations of the wood throughout the rod, it was possible to cast enormous distances with little effort, and it is unknown for a rod in good condition to break. The invention took the angling world by storm, particularly after Grant achieved a world record cast of almost 55 yards at a competition held at Wimbeldon in 1896. Grant had patented his invention two years earlier, and at this time was making rods single-handed in his workshop above his hairdresser's shop at 4 Baron Taylor's Lane (now Street), Inverness. However, in 1900, when he could no longer cope with the demand for them, he sold his patent to Messrs, Playfair of Aberdeen. From this time on, his creative efforts were centred on improving the quality of his fiddles, a task which had first aroused his interest in the early 1880s.

In 1887, Alexander Grant opened a shop in Inverness as a fishing rod and tackle maker. He fished the Ness but sometimes broke his rod when casting for far out fish. Looking for a solution, Grant recalled his discovery of the 'thread of vibration' when experimenting with the thickness of violin plates. This led him to develop an *acoustic method* for determining the taper of a fishing rod. The result was a rod which behaved like a newly cut sapling: flexible, almost unbreakable and every part springing in unison.

At the same time, Grant patented a *lap joint* which was non-slipping and allowed the rod to bend (and twist) as if it were made from a 'single' piece of wood.

Grant abhorred 'shooting the line'. Instead, he would pay out as much line as he needed then, using a *switch cast of his own devising*, loop it upstream and throw it out to wherever he wanted.

With upright eyes, Grant noticed that, at a point in the backward loop of his cast, slack line near the tip of the rod caused the line to loop back down the eyes. Tacking up this slack in the forward throw reduced the effectiveness of the cast. *Fall-down eyes* on the rod fixed the problem.

The Rondello

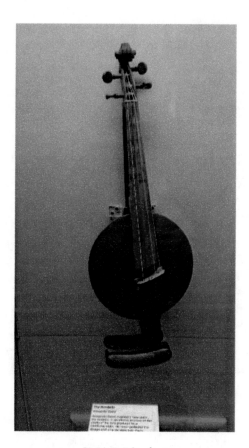

IMAG Display

Grant believed that the main shortcoming of the traditional fiddle shape lay in the fact that it had so many obstacles to the free vibration of the wood, such as the f-holes, and side bites (to allow for bowing), and that "while these exist no true tone can be produced. The tones you hear are simply over-tones blended, and not the full and true tones which can be produced on the new violin – tones nearer the human voice than can be produced on any other fiddle". The new "violin" to which he refers is his invention – the Rondello. This instrument, with its distinctive shape, is such a complete break with the traditional design as to justify Scott Skinner's description of him as "genius and inventor". The instrument is hollow throughout, including the neck, all braces and supports. Inside, a series of sound-posts, arranged in a circle around the perimeter of the sound hole, transfer the vibrations from the front of the instrument to the back. In the Rondello, each tiny part, including the distinctive bridge, has been designed and made by Grant himself.

The Highland Strathspey and Reel Society

Grant was the leader of the Society from its inception. It was founded in 1903 by a group of Inverness gentlemen with the aim of reviving "public interest in the old dance music of Scotland and of cultivating the art of playing this music on the fiddle". He continued as leader for almost 40 years, by which time he had become widely referred to as "The Scott Skinner of the Highlands". He also composed his own tunes, two of which are still played regularly by the Society, "Scott Skinners Welcome to Inverness", a march published in 1924, and "Donald Morison", a strathspey named after a Society member and assistant who was another close friend of Skinners.

Highland Strathspey and Reel Orchestra

Grant seated, 2nd left

Donald Morison was the owner of Morisons Ironmonger, Beauly. The shop still serves much the same purpose from when it was taken over by the current Donald Fraser's father. There is a small display of memorabilia, correspondence and a unique Alexander Battan Grant violin passed on to the Fraser family held in a small upstairs pitch pine panelled room. The

20

photograph of this violin which has been used throughout this book was taken by Donald's daughter Laura. In addition to a portrait of Scott Skinner there is also Scott Skinner's will – displayed in a small frame hanging on the wall. The portrait is identical to that shown hanging in Grants living room in part 2 of this book – indeed it may be the same one.

The tradition represented by Alexander Grant was fortunately carried on by Society member, Donald Riddell, who became assistant leader under him in 1931, and who also learnt from him the art of fiddle making. His achievements and the legacy which he passed on are presented in parts 3 and 4. Post war, the leadership of the Society was taken on by Grant's pupil Donald Riddell, Pipe Major in the Lovat Scouts, and crofter on the Lovat Estates.

The bulk of this text has been compiled from Leaflet 2006 held in the Museum's possesion and is attributed to Graeme Farnell.

<Graeme Farnell -

Past Curator of Inverness Museum gratefully acknowledged the assistance of Miss M. Grant, Mr D. Riddell, and Mrs D. B. Spankie.>

<Sinclair Gair –

Acknowledges:

Donald Fraser, Morisons Ironmonger's, Main Street, Beauly, for introducing me to the past history and achievements of Alexander Battan Grant, and for letting me have a look at the memorabilia belonging to Grant, Donald Morrison and Scott Skinner on display in the shop. Donald's assertion 'that the man deserves to be better known' was the catalyst which drove me to produce this book.

Kari Moody, Curator at IMAG, for giving me access to all of the Museums written records and for allowing me to photograph the contents of Grants workshop held in the Museum's store room.

The assistance of George McIntosh of Grantown-on-Spey in locating Battangorm croft ….all highland fiddlers owe us two accordionists a debt of gratitude>.

Alexander 'Battan' Grant

1856 - 1942

(His Life and Legacy)

Part 2

A compilation of Grant's Life History

Alexander Grant

(Studio Portrait)

Introduction

Alexander Grant was born in 1856 at Battangorm Croft Carrbridge, (Battan becoming the name that he was most popularly known by). He remained there for the following fifteen years of his life before moving to Garbole, Dalarossie, Upper Findhorn, with his brother Charles. Historical records indicate that the family had a long previous association with Battangorm with many relatives spread throughout the local area. Alexander's father James [James died on the 18th February, 1892 at Battangorm] and his mother Marjory [Rose, Duthil] between them had twelve children one infant was still born, Helen who died after seven days, Mary at 5 years, and two other sisters, Margaret and Ann who lived to the ages of 85 and 77 respectively.

Of his six brothers, James who married Margaret Calder [Gorbals], lived and worked locally with their ten children in Carrbridge had his occupation listed as butcher and shepherd. Charles married Isabella Darroch from Govan [two children], and lived in Kingussie, working as a policeman and shepherd, died aged 87 and played the pipes. His brother David died in Petroria, South Africa, age about 33 years, of entric fever, was single and a Pipe Major in the Cameronians. Of his remaining three brothers, John, Peter and William all of whom at some time or another emigrated to, or worked in Australia. It was William however who featured in Alexander's life at a later date through an involvement in a financial investment scheme. The scheme did not make any profit business wise, and a further loss was incurred upon redeeming the shares upon the death of William due to the devaluation of the pound. William who was two years younger than Alexander remained single and died in his 70's. He is reputed to have invented a means of making paper from esparto grass, went to New Zealand then Australia and played the sock market. He part owned Edna May gold mine in Kalgoorlie and returned to Scotland to raise money in 1926/27. It would have been about this time that Alexander invested in one of his schemes. This is stated in one of Alexanders letters to his nephew (name unknown) and reproduced at the end of this chapter. On his death he left his fortune to his sister Margaret – listed as being a gold and water deviner(!) who was single, lived in Inverness and died age eighty five.

It was in 1886 having previously moved to Dalarossie with his brother Charles that Grant made a fiddle [his first?]. Following on from which in 1887 he announced his move to Inverness to start up business in Glenalbyn Building, Young Street, as a fishing tackle maker. By this stage of his life his skills with a fishing rod became apparent having the same year caught a 55lb salmon on the river Garry in September. His move to Inverness and his close proximity to the river Ness must have been for him a marriage made in heaven. He must have either been extremely gifted, or spent many hours practicing, or both, for him to realise the short commings of the rods that he was using. This subsequently led him to successfully patent his ideas and make a considerable sum of money from the eventual sale of his patent. The name 'Grant's Vibration Rod' is still in use today when anyone refers to his design of a Greenheart fishing rod.

In 1890 Grant began a long and close friendship with the renowned fiddler, James Scott Skinner. So much so that on marrying his wife Elizabeth (Bessie) Kennedy, Edinburgh [29th January 1891], he christened his first son James Scott Skinner [born 11th November 1891].

This, in turn, through his methodical habit of recording and storing information has led to the preservation of a considerable volume of correspondence from Skinner. Skinner unfortunately did not do likewise with the result that anyone researching J. S. Skinner [died 1927] would do well to consult the historical record of Alexander Grant.

At the outset of this book, it was only the authors intention to research the historical records of Alexander Grant. However, the closeness of Grant's association with Skinner has led to the inclusion of all of this one sided information flow as it relates to Grant. Furthermore, a lineage from Donald Riddell, Donald Morison and his pupils creates a clear time line which ends with Riddell's pupils who are performing today, notably Duncan Chisholm, and Bruce MacGregor. For this reason a very clear picture has emerged of the importance of Alexander Grant's influence on the cultural heritage of the Highlands which can be given prominence – the task now being to raise awareness and build upon these achievements for the benefit of today's and future generations of young musicians.

In 1892 Grant's deep interest in violin-making and his determination to improve its sound qualities was brought to light when he produced a guitar-shaped fiddle. This instrument is today on view in Inverness Museum and is illustrated in Part 1. However, his interests in the vibratory properties of wood also led him to improve the durability and effectiveness of fishing rods – particularly those made from Green Hart wood. On the 28th May, 1894, he applied for a Patent (No. 10,385) relating to 'spliced joint for fishing rod'. His application was handled by Johnsons Patent Office, Glasgow. His application was accepted on the 4th May, 1895 and the Grant Vibration Rod was born. He had immediate success with his invention and his name and casting abilities with it became well known. So much so that he was invited to demonstrate his new rod's casting capabilities on December 10, 11, and 12th, 1896 to a select fishing audience at Kingston-on-Thames. Editors of "The Field" and "Land & Water" were present and he proceeded to out-cast all of his competitors. Further proof of his rods capabilities were noted with respect to the fact that Grant was not a big man, being of smallish light build and did not possess a large physical frame. In the passing of time others have claimed to beat his casting feat. However they have not achieved this using his casting method - *so his record still stands to this day*.

In 1900, he sold his business in Baron Taylors Lane (Fishing Tackle Maker, Tin/Coppersmith, Hairdresser), and unable to meet the demand for his Vibration rod sold his splice patent to Charles Playfair, Aberdeen, for £100 pounds. (The name Playfair still trades to this day as a company supplying the highest class Premium sporting guns and rifles, and owner of Purdy – thee top class manufacturer of shot guns and rifles of various calibers which are sold throughout the world).

Battangorm Croft

Typical of the croft houses built pre 1880's with peat tiles and wood roof timbers - which were usually taken by the resident(s) when moving their place of dwelling.

Battangorm Croft - Marjory Grant, Sandy's mother, in

'Widows weeds' knitting a sock

(Grant's mother died on the 5th October 1916 at Dalnansyde cottage, Carrbridge - his daughter Mary's house).

Part of the croft lands can still be seen between the railway line and the old road to Inverness - "battan" (or "baddan") means clump or small cluster; "gorm" means blue-green. The site of the house and steading lie slightly under the main road to the west of the burn, but no remains are visible because the stones were taken away to build a house in Carrbridge. This house was originally called Alderdale but, coincidentally, in the 1990s called Baddengorm. (See following map).

The croft had a thatched, hipped roof and the 1881 and 1891 Census's confirm that it had two rooms and only two windows. The drawing (below) of a croft house was instantly recognised by Alexander Battan Grant's daughter, Madge Grant (1899 to 1996), who remembered the place from her youth. She confirmed that it had an earthen floor and that the peat fire never went out.

Sandy's mother in her late years

Battangorm was abandoned sometime after 1905. James (Marjory's/Jame's son), who ran a butcher's business initially from Battangorm [Mary, illegitimate daughter of Sandy Battan and grand mother of Michael Kerr (78 at the time of writing - see later) could remember the awful task of cleaning out the insides of sheep in the burn]. He subsequently moved with his family to Carrbridge while his mother moved further up the burn to a wooden cottage reputedly bought for her by her son Sandy. The cottage, erected as a hospital when the railway was being built in the 1890s, (accidents when building the railways were not an uncommon occurrence) is today replaced by a modern house (although offset from the cottage site).

A house of the style of Battangorm

The above was instantly recognized as Battangorm by someone who knew it well. However, the proceeding photograph shows that Battangorm had a roof made of peat 'tiles' (not reeds as shown above), a chimney probably positioned nearer the end rather than the middle of the roof and a tiny, recessed porch. [Note from Michael Kerr – *Great Grandson of Sandy Battan* - 'we know the proceeding photograph is of Battangorm because: it came from a family source; it shows Marjory (Rose) Grant sitting outside the doorway and we know from other photographs what she looked like]. Battangorm had only two rooms and two windows (1891 Census), and was a logical development of the turf-sided house style of Strathspey. However, some drawings of the time are probably in error by showing a thatch of reeds because the photograph of Battangorm reveals that the thatch used in the Duthil area was, in fact, made of peat tiles.

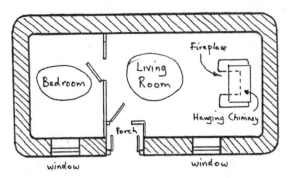

Schematic plan layout of a typical Speyside Croft

The hanging fireplace of a turf-sided house as illustrated in, (and courtesy of), **Highland Folk Ways by Isobel Grant.** Stone-built up to about 3 feet with a wooden canopy above to take the smoke out of the roof. Battangorm would have had such a fireplace but probably attached to the roof near one end of the living room.

An example of a barn roof support system using both wall supports and crucks

Battangorm's all-stone walls were held together with mortar and the roof probably rested on the walls rather than on Crucks (Michael's deduction – however see below). Inside, the floor was earthen and the roof space was open the length of the house (no ceiling). A peat fire, which never went out, warmed the whole house and helped preserve the roof. Carrbridge still has a good example of this type of house in nearby Bog Roy, but it now has harled walls and a red corrugated iron roof.

The Croft house with exterior porch, three windows, central chimney dating from the time of Battangorm – which is about half a mile further up the road, (+ man's best friend)
(© Sinclair Gair)

The Croft house interior (fire-place positioned towards one end of the room) - dating

Lengths of wood strapping (painted white) have been slid in above the crucks and below the thatch material which is still in place. The red corrugated roof panels have been laid on top of the thatch, some of which is visible from within the croft.

The original crucks – thought to be about 300 years old
(© Sinclair Gair)

Location of Battangorm Croft and School House shown center

Possible Connection with the Lairds of Grant (later the Seafields)

Background family history research carried out by Michael Kerr, great grandson of Alexander 'Battan' Grant (see later), has uncovered an intriguing link to the Lairds of Grant.

James Grant, Sandy Battan's father

In Michael Kerr's words:

It seems that we are descended, albeit via an illegitimate birth, from the Seafields. One James Grant [carpenter – not the one in the photograph], is probably the "natural" son of James Grant of Grant then living at Castle Grant and known as the "Good Sir James".

Note: "Natural" was the term used for the illegitimate offspring of the gentry; "born in fornication" was the term used for the peasantry.

What is the evidence for the connection?

1. There has always been a strong family rumour about it.
2. Marjory Grant (1899 – 1996), daughter of Alex Grant (Sandy "Battan") and grand daughter of James Grant [tailor – the one in the photograph], confirmed it (about 1989) without giving the connection except that "it was a long way back". The Seafield lawyer's were supposed to have approached Alex Grant about it at one time.
3. The Peoples Journal of 15th Mar, 1897, carried a very informative article of the life of Alex Grant (Sandy "Battan"), son of James Grant [tailor]. The story is so detailed that only Alex himself could have supplied the facts. The article hints at his lineage back to the Laird of Grant in the oblique, reverential way Victorians reported any scandal involving the high born. (Whatever the gentry got up to was beyond reproach and put above the understanding of ordinary folk!)…"*Mr Grant is a native of Strathspey, being born in the Parish of Duthil, about one and a half miles from Carr Bridge….where his*

aged mother still resides, his forfathers having the right of clan descent granted them by the Chiefs of the Grants to abide there. Mr Grant's father (now deceased) used to remark his remembering when his father's holding [of Battangorm] was free. A moiety is now charged to establish the legal right of the proprietor, but the fact proves his family to have had honour with the chiefs of the clan in olden times."

4. Lady Caroline, who died in 1911, made special visits to Battangorm to see James Grant [tailor]. My grandmother (Alex Grant's illegitimate daughter Mary), who was brought up at Battangorm, can remember these visits [when other family members were asked to wait outside], which confirm that James Grant [tailor] was a "somebody". (The gentry were not given to calling on small crofters).

    "Natural" children and their descendants were "looked after" in case the legitimate family died out which in a way it did for the Seafields because, in 1881, Caroline inherited the Grant and Seafield estates from her only child, Ian Charles, when he died suddenly without issue. The barony of Grant became "extinct" because the title could only pass down the male line (the Seafield title, in contrast, could, and did, come down the female side).

    This may explain something my grandmother overheard James Grant [tailor] saying to Lady Caroline, "Naw, naw, Caroline, I hope it doesn't happen in my time." Lady Caroline was also supposed to have offered to build James a new house but his reply was, "Naw, Caroline, this'll do me fine."

5. My mother told me that, when she was in Austrailia in the early 1940's, John and Peter, the oldest and youngest sons of James [tailor], both confirmed that Battangorm had been given to the family by the Grant estate.

Castle Grant, the home of the 'good' Sir James

near Granton on Spey

How was it possible for an illegitimate son of the Laird of Grant to become connected with the Grants of Inschtomach/Battangorm? [Inschtomach – the ruins of this croft are still visible on the Foregin hill side, near Carrbridge, and is in the general area of where Battangorm croft was located].

Here is a plausible scenario, starting with a curious entry in the Inverallan (Grantown) parish records:

William Dunbar squarewright [a carpenter] in Grantown and his spouse Margaret had a child baptised (James) 14th April 1787 which was neglected to be registered by Mr Piery [name unclear] late schoolmaster of Cromdale.
Witness names:
    James Grant, son to Sir James Grant of Grant,
    [Sir James' son would have been about 11 years old at the time.]
    James Seton, stocking weaver in Grantown.

"Had a child baptised" is unusual wording for a baptismal entry in a parish register – there is no feeling of parental connection. Also, why was it "neglected" to be registered? And what was the Laird's son doing attending the baptism of an ordinary worker's son? Could it be that he was attending the baptism of his half-brother under orders from the castle? If the child took his REAL father's surname, and if he later took up the trade of his adopted father, then we have a good fit for James Grant [carpenter], {as detailed in an associated document produced by Michael Kerr – 'The Grants'}. It would be natural for James Grant [carpenter], and therefore, itinerant to migrate from Grantown to Duthil where recent agricultural improvements were creating a demand for better buildings.

Caroline, Countess of Seafield
(On the untimely death in 1884 of her son, Ian Charles, 8th Earl of Seafield,
the Countess continued to administer the Seafield estates.)

[Authors note: Michael, it has to be said, has produced a note-worthy volume of investigative results on his family tree, giving precise detail of his forebear's genealogy. His efforts stand out as a very well researched piece of work, worthy of any scolarly activity.

However, a further interesting observation which Michael would not have consulted takes us to the correspondence addressed to Grant from Skinner. In numerous letters to Grant, Skinner was in the habit of prefixing Grant's name with terminology such as: The Tomnahurich Genius; Genius of the Century; The Edison of the North; Brave Battan; and most intriguingly of all – 'Chief of Clan Grant'. It is likely that the mis-deeds of the Gentry would have been well-known to the small community of Duthil (especially if a new offspring appeared and no woman locally was known to have been pregnant!). Such stories would have been passed down and quite possibly Grant himself would have at some stage of their friendship have mentioned the possibility to Skinner – as stated in point 3 above when he most likely gave the interview to the The Peoples Journal of 15th March, 1897].

**Jim Grant (Sandy's eldest son) with cousin Willie Anderson
at railway hospital, Battangorm**

The old railway hospital building became the house of Grant's mother after Battangorm croft deteriorated and was no longer fit for human habitation, around 1905. The stones were later removed to build a house in nearby Carrbridge – just behind the pub.

Historic Note: One hundred and thirty five years previously, during Samuel Johnson's, (the author of the first English Dictionary), grand tour of Scotland in the early 1770's, he described houses of this type as:

"A hut is constructed of loose stones, ranged for the most part with some tendency to circularity. It must be placed where the wind cannot act upon it with violence, because it has no cement; and where the water will run easily away, because it has no floor but the naked ground. The wall, which is commonly about six feet high, declines from the perpendicular a little inward. Such rafters as can be procured are then raised for a roof, and covered with heath, which makes a strong and warm thatch, kept from flying off by ropes of twisted heath, of which the ends, reaching from the centre of the thatch to the top of the wall, are held firm by the weight of a large stone. These stones hang round the bottom of the roof, and make it look like a lady's hair in papers. No light is admitted but at the entrance, and through a hole in the thatch, which gives vent to the smoke. This hole is not directly over the fire, lest the rain should extinguish it, and the smoke therefore naturally fills the place before it escapes. Huts however are no more uniform than palaces".

Clearly not much had changed in the intervening years.

Alexander Battan Grant – A Profile and History of his Life

Sandy Grant (early 20's)

"Sandy Battan" had a variety of occupations and no little fame throughout his lifetime. The Census of 1861 and 1871 finds him home at Battangorm. In the following years, Sandy tried his hand as an apprentice draper in Wales, a forester at Cullen (but had to quit due to a burst blood vessel in the lungs) and a grocer/butcher in Carrbridge. In 1881, he was a grocer at Garbole, Strathdearn (several miles up the River Findhorn from Tomatin) and also did some hairdressing. Here he had a liaison with a local farmer's daughter and ended up getting her pregnant. The farmer thwarted marriage and forced Sandy to accept custody of the baby, a daughter, born 1883. He then returned to Battangorm. By this time in his life, Sandy was an expert on fishing and fishing tackle, so he tried large scale fly making in the winter and switched to being a ghillie in the fishing season, (in most years for Lord Burton of Dochfour, Dochdarrach, Loch Ness). In 1887, Sandy moved from Carrbridge to Inverness, leaving his daughter, Mary, in the care of his parents. He started a fishing tackle business in Glenalbyn Building, Young St, but, as this brought insufficient income, he added hairdressing. About a year or two later, he moved his premises to 7 Baron Taylor's Lane and, about 1892, he invented the Grant Vibration rod, the consequences of which changed his life forever.

Alexander Battan Grant, 7 Baron Taylor's Lane, Inverness

(standing, centre, in doorway)

Sandy's Great Grandson Michael Kerr

standing at the same spot, May 2019

(The shop is easily identifiable even today)

(© Sinclair Gair)

Having moved in 1906, his final occupation was as a farmer at Tomnahurich Farm, which during the time before housing development encroachment lay just outside Inverness.

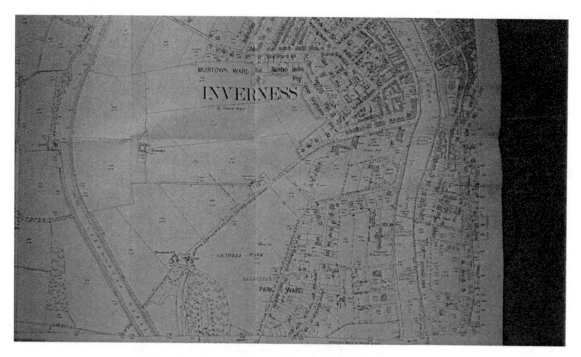

Tomnahurich Farm – bottom at the base of the hill

His Legacy

Sandy's unique heritage derives from becoming well-known in Scotland, the UK and abroad in two separate fields: fishing and music, in which for a man of his time, he made seminal contributions. He mastered for himself most of the skills he acquired, and the discoveries he made, in fishing and fiddling. Despite his unassuming nature, these achievements attracted the attention and admiration of the experts. In other words, his achievements could not be ignored by his peer group of knowledgeable people who were at the forefront of the developments in both these fields.

His Main Achievements:

On fishing he was regarded as:

- An inventor of a fishing rod with almost magical casting capabilities and a skilled craftsman at actually making the rods. Inverness museum has a collection of his rods (although apart from one, they are not normally on display).

- Among other things, Sandy also invented the "Planet" cast, a simplification and a vast improvement of the Spey cast, (and recently reconstructed and demonstrated by Gordon MacCleod, a Gillie on Speyside).

- A man whose practical and technical abilities in fishing were recognised as that of a master. Jock Scott, the noted author on fishing, for example, wrote articles and the book "Fine and Far Off" – dedicated to Sandy, about his record casts and his complete skills as a fisherman. Sandy belongs to that small group of people who have caught a salmon weighing more than 50 pounds weight; and he once caught a salmon on the Ness at a recorded distance of 47 yards.

- With his all-round knowledge, experience and expertise in all departments, Sandy could well claim to be the most complete salmon fisher ever. However, fame was never uppermost in his mind, and he never really troubled himself with the claims made by others less competent. [Sandy Battan's outstanding fishing legacy and achievements are detailed in the book 'Alexander Battan Grant – His Life and Legacy', by the author].

On fiddle playing and violin making, he was regarded as:

- A very good violinist and a master player of Scottish music. His friend James Scott Skinner recognised his ability in fiddle playing, particularly the bowing of Highland music. "Where did you learn to play like that?" Skinner asked Sandy when they first met at a concert in Inverness (supposedly 1890), "Gie me your right hand and I'll gie you mine."

- In addition to being a top class solo player, Sandy along with other fiddlers founded and led the Highland Strathspey and Reel Society in 1903. The Society was regarded as one of the best in Scotland, and he led it from its founding till near his death in 1942. (The Society, as noted elsewhere, was from around 1931 subsequently led by Donald Riddell).

- A maker of violins of exceptionally neat workmanship and sweet tone. He obtained the good tone by tapping the plates and acoustically balancing them, i.e. making them, in some sense, acoustically identical.

- Inverness Museum has a display case featuring some of his fiddles, including a Rondello (a round disc shaped fiddle which was ultimately a failure). One of his fiddles now belongs to Donald Fraser at Donald Morisons Ironmongers in Beauly from whom it was passed on, and is illustrated throughout this book.

Grant accompanied by Madge MacKenzie, an aunt of Michael Kerr

To help his rod and tackle business, Sandy became a well-known and ardent fisher of the Ness and worked fervently making rods. His invention of the Grant Vibration rod was driven by the need to reach distant fish on the river which, of course, is very wide. His achievement was to make a rod that behaved like a newly cut sapling before it dries out (he had noticed the difference as a boy). Many people think that the performance of the rod came from its lap joint, for which Sandy took out a patent (Patent No 10,385: applied for 28 May 1894, accepted 4 May 1895), but the real secret of the rod is its taper, which was worked out acoustically, rod by rod. The lap joint simply allowed the rod to behave as if it were made in one piece (other joint arrangements either do not bend and/or are points of weakness). It is no exaggeration to say that the Grant Vibration rod "blew away" the standards set by other fly rods and, in the late 1890s, it caused much controversy amongst the "experts" on fly casting, (see the voluminous correspondence in the fishing and sporting magazines of the time).

Sandy Grant (2nd left)

Demonstration of the Grant Vibration rod on the River Ness,

below the Ness islands at the fishermen's shelter

Sandy initially made the rods himself in Baron Taylor's Lane, (now Street), Inverness, where he was also a barber. In 1900, he sold the design rights of the rod for £100 plus a royalty for every rod sold from 1900 to 1910 to John and Charles Robb of Playfairs, Aberdeen, who made the rods up until the arrival of modern rod making methods and materials (in around the 1960s). As far as is known, Playfairs did not use the acoustic principle but simply copied the masters rods very accurately. Since the characteristics of Greenheart is fairly consistent, a "copied" rod performs as well or nearly as well as a "real" one. When it was made, the Grant Vibration rod was 'THE' salmon fishing rod. Being the (near) perfect rod, it still performs better than modern rods but is much more expensive to make and heavier. The rod, together with a tapered line, can be likened to a long, perfectly balanced bull whip.

The agreement for the sale of the rights to the rod is short:

(Grant's letter to Playfair)

> *Baron Taylor's Lane*
>
> *20 Aug 1900*
>
> *Inverness*

Gents

I accept the sum of one hundred pounds Stg £100 for –

Firstly, My Patent No 10,385 viz. A non slipping splice for fishing rods

golf club handles and other like articles.

Secondly, My secret method of manufacture and wood treatment employed by me in the making of my vibration rod.

Thirdly, My registered ring used in connection with my vibration rod.

Fourthly, The sole right and power to make and sell my vibration rod.

Further I accept your undertaking to pay me a royalty of 10% on the net price of every vibration rod made and sold by your firm from 1ˢᵗ Sept 1900 until 1 Sept 1910.

All rods made by you to be numbered consecutively from No 1.

Yours faithfully

Alex Grant

After selling the rights, Sandy did not give up rod making. Correspondence with the Robbs shows that he helped Playfairs for many years afterwards, initially to get them up and running with the peculiarities of the rod but later to do specials or sort problems. In 1902, he built a workshop specifically for rod making but, unfortunately, it was completely destroyed by fire in May or June - only 3 weeks after its completion. Nothing was insured. (Michael Kerr – 'My grandmother told me that his sons, Jock and Willie, started the fire accidentally').

Correspondence makes clear that Sandy gave up active fishing for good about the time he sold the patent. He turned his mind to exploring the vibration principle in general and to its application to the violin in particular. Other pressures at the time might have been his founding, with others, of the Strathspey and Reel Society in 1903 and his take up of the tenancy of Tomnahurich farm in 1906.

Sandy was very disappointed with Playfairs' lackadaisical handling of the Vibration rod. He was particularly infuriated by the replacement of his fall down eyes with rigid upright eyes, and Playfairs' lack of drive in getting suitable tapered lines made for the rods (essential to its optimum performance). A quote from a draft letter to Charles Robb highlights his annoyance:

"Had you persisted in what I fought for single handed [in the 1890s] against all opposition in both art and execution, today there would be a different story to tell when you could rest on your own oars and pull as desired, [just] as I did and [be able to] laugh out all the Hardies in existence."

[In the 1890s, after the rod - and Sandy's prowess with it - hit the fishing world, a vociferous opposition, led by Hardie of fishing tackle fame, tried vainly to discredit him and the rod.]

Although brought up by a mother who was a very sincere Presbyterian, Sandy later became an avowed atheist and didn't hold back in trying to convert others (a brave thing to do in his day). [Michael Kerr – 'an uncle of mine told me what made him switch beliefs. Apparently, Sandy was struggling with the concept or an aspect of the vibration rod, so he prayed and prayed to God for the answer. The solution to the problem came to him while he was cutting somebody's hair. He reckoned that he had worked it out for himself and that God had not bothered to answer him. I did not understand the story until I found out about the fervent religious atmosphere that existed in Duthil in the time of Sandy's youth ("Duthil Past and Present" by the Rev Donald Maclean published by James Thin, 1910). In those times, God was expected to answer your prayers in a very dramatic, vivid way - like writing on the wall'].

Sandy married Elizabeth Kennedy in 1892 in Edinburgh (a letter his brother wrote to him in 1897 confirms that Sandy knew her from his time in Strathdearn). She bore him 6 children, James, Ann, John and William at 4 Ardross Place and Marjory and Alexander in Rowan Bank, Ballifeary Road. His first daughter Mary came to stay with them in the mid 1890s and was there for the 1901 Census. His oldest son's middle names, "Scott Skinner", was in honour of the famous fiddler, now his new pal.

Elizabeth ("Bessie") Grant, nee Kennedy, Grant's wife

Proof of Grant's everlasting contribution to:

The Cultural Legacy of the Highlands

Grants memorabilia shown in the centre and right hand display panels at

Inverness Museum and Art Gallery (IMAG)

(© Sinclair Gair)

Grant's great grandson Michael Kerr
(A violinist and instrument maker – May 2019, IMAG)
(© Sinclair Gair)

Examples of Grant's work (© Sinclair Gair)

Michael holds one of Grant's Rondello's (© Sinclair Gair)

Grant persevered with the Rondello for most of his life, but in the end had to admit that the Italian model was best. (© Sinclair Gair)

Grant's attempt at making a Roncello

(Quote from Grant - 'It will take celloist's to their knees and never again

touch their empty spurious tinpot noise boxes again').

(© Sinclair Gair)

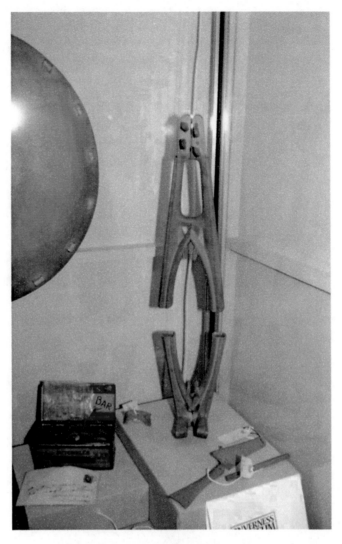

Frame for a Rondello, and storage tin

Grant was meticulous in every thing he did. Small items were placed in tins which were then grouped in larger tins for storage. No one, not even his best friends, were ever allowed into his upstairs workshop. (An interesting voice recording of Donald Riddell telling this story exists on the Ambaile website - www.ambaile.org.uk).

Grant made several Rondello's of which

possibly only two have survived

Some of the contents of Grant's workshop

which were bequeathed to the museum

The Formation of the first Highland Strathspey & Reel Society - 1903

STRATHSPEY & REEL ORCHESTRA. INVERNESS.

The Highland Strathspey and Reel Society in the 1920's

(Formed by Grant as its leader in 1903)

Standing: Mr Wheatley; _____; Mr Tom Gordon (Engine Driver); Mr Willie MacKay; Mr Duncan Grant (Watchmaker); Mr George Bell (Butcher); Mr Jim MacBean (Culcabock); Mr D.W. Call (Burgh Assessor for nearly 50 years). Sitting: Mr Alex Grant (Leader of the Society); Mr Duncan MacKenzie; Mr John Fraser; Mr Donald Riddell (became leader of the Society in 1973).

(Courtesy of Inverness Field Club – Old Inverness in Pictures)

A group at the Strathspey and Reel Dinner

Back Row: Mr William (Treasurer and Fire Master); Mr A. Duffie; Mr James MacKenzie; ____; Front Row: Mr Tom MacPherson; Mr John Fraser; Mr D.W. Call; Mr Alex Grant.

(Courtesy of Inverness Field Club – Old Inverness in Pictures)

File No. *33730.*
193*6.*

.... *22 JUN 1937* .... 193 .

From

Section 10 (Entertainments Duty),
Secretaries' Office,
Custom House,
London, E.C. 3.

To

J. Fraser, Esq.,

....

....

Sir,

The Highland Strathspey & Reel Society

With reference to the exemption from Entertainments Duty granted
to the above organisation in respect of the entertainment held
on ..... *10th July, 1936.* ...., I am to remind you that,
if exemption is required in respect of any similar entertainment to
be given during the present season, application (giving particulars
of the date and place) must be made to this Office, in accordance
with No. 15 (1) of the Entertainments Duty Regulations, 1921, not
less than fourteen days prior to the entertainment. The application
should be accompanied by a copy of the last annual financial
statement of the organisation covering all its activities, a
detailed programme of the entertainment (a proof or manuscript copy
will suffice) and a statement whether there has been any change in
the rules, constitution or circumstances of the organisation since
exemption was last granted.

Secretary

We frequently complain about modern day bureaucracy - but would traditional music concerts have survived if this level of income tax scrutiny had continued?

Highland Strathspey & Reel Society 1935 – Alexander 'Battan' Grant holding cap.

Donald Morison, assistant leader, is in the front row, with glasses

(Courtesy of Inverness Field Club – Old Inverness in Pictures)

Donald Morison – First Assistant leader of the Highland Strathspey & Reel Society (1903)

Donald Morison, as far as is known, spent his entire life in Beauly, having inherited his father Roderick's, Ironmonger's business. The layout of the town square today remains as it was in Morison's day, but would have looked considerably different in detail. In his childhood, and before the advent of motorised transport, he would have been very well accustomed to walking through it, as shown here, with no defined roadway surface and no pavements.

Beauly Square towards the end of the nineteenth century.

Morisons Ironmongers is located at the far end of the road going East (SSE).

(Photograph here, and the following six sourced from the Facebook page 'Memories of Beauly' archive. Administered and hosted by Muriel Campbell of Beauly in 2020).

The Square, Beauly.

Looking West (NNW), the Priory Hotel at the opposite end of the square was sited

in front of the ruins of the Augustine Priory Monastery

(Courtesy of George Washington collection, University of Edinburgh)

For Donald Morison, walking through this square in the 1890's, (approximate date of photograph), would have been an every-day experience. His father's shop remains as it is today only 50 yards before reaching this point. The (now) former Royal Bank of Scotland building sits behind the railings on the right-hand side - he would likely even have known the names of the children shown here. (The now former Bank of Scotland building is situated directly opposite – a sign of how the banking industry was forced to change in the way it served its customers in the 'digital revolution' following on from the 1998 financial collapse of many banks).

At a later time, 1905, the appearance of the square was transformed with the erection of the Lovat Scout Monument.

THE SQUARE, BEAULY (EAST END)

The West end of the Square – post 1905 (Postcard in error – '<u>not</u> the East end')

Founded by Simon the 14th Lord Lovat and twenty-second Chief of the Clan Fraser of Lovat, raised Lovat's Scouts (later known as the Lovat Scouts) early in the year 1900 to fight in the South African Boer War - 'A Chief among his own people and leader of a thousand warriors'. The family name in Gaelic has been MacShimidh (the son of Simon) from time immemorial.

'Historic Note: In earlier times, large landowners (clan chiefs), and well-to-do gentry, raised small army's in defence of the country's interests - including their own. Long before 1900, the 78th Fraser Highlanders were raised in 1757 by Simon Fraser of Lovat to fight against the French in Canada. They assisted General Wolfe at the siege of Quebec, the capture of Montreal, and finally Canada was surrendered to the British. The regiments actions are still re-enacted in Quebec to this day. Having only existed for about six years, and some of this abroad, this was in recompense for the Frasers having found themselves on the wrong side during the 2nd Jacobite rising. This was the first stage of re-patriation of the Lovat Estates by proving loyalty to the Crown. The 2nd Battalion is still known (locally), to this day, as having comprised 'bowl o' meal' Frasers. Crofters and members of different clans willing to change their surname for what was basically an inducement by means of food - thereby making it appear that all of the Fraser clan were 'on board' with this allegiance.

Over time, many Highland Regiments combined with one another or were disbanded, thus we have as possibilities the 78th Highland Regiment of foot (Seaforth's) 1778, amalgamated with the 72nd Highland Regiment of foot in 1809, and with the 72nd of foot (Duke of Albany's own Highlanders) in 1823. There was another unit, the 71st Regiment of foot raised in 1775 for the American revolutionary war and known as Fraser Highlanders. In 1881 the 72nd (Duke of Albany's own Highlanders – known as the Ross-shire Buffs) Regiment of foot, amalgamated under the banner of the Seaforth Highlanders. Quite a confusing picture with their own stories/histories attached.

Additionally, apart from military historic evolutionary developments, the rifle range in Beauly was used for training by the Lovat Scouts during their summer camps, (though it is thought that few would have needed it). Prior to that, some of the units mentioned above, operating under the banner of the Seaforth's, also used this rifle range. [see 'A Metal Detecting Survey of Beauly Fields', by E. Soame, North of Scotland Archaeology Society]'.

Simon Joseph was brought up at Beaufort Castle the family home near Beauly in Inverness-shire. The earliest mention of the site, as Downie or Dounie castle, occurs in the reign of Alexander 1, (1106 – 1224) of Scotland. The current castle construction was built in 1882 and badly damaged by fire in 1935. It is believed a stray spark from a small chimney fire that had burnt some five days previously landed on the dry duck-boarding of Beaufort's roof and smouldered; then crept along the whole of one wing until a guest of wind ignited it. The first anyone in the building knew of impending disaster was when two boys who had been playing on the green ran into the courtyard shouting, 'The Castle's on fire' and by that time the whole wing was blazing. The only reason the Castle was not burnt to the ground was that the wind suddenly changed direction and blew back over the part that was already gutted.

Unveiling the Lovat Scout monument 1905 - all wearing caps in respect

of the significance of the occasion. (Could Donald Morison have been in this crowd?)

However, this beautiful view of the square was drastically altered by fire in 1913.

The burnt-out shell of the Beauly Priory Hotel, 1913. The building was not finally demolished until 1923.

The square was naturally a focal point for the local community and important gatherings and events were held there.

The Highland Light Infantry (HLI) marching past the Lovat monument on the 28/07/19(?)
(Note: the hand written date on this post card is likely to be in error – see above)

At a later time, Morisons ironmonger business passed through the Ellis family into the ownership of the current Donald Fraser's father.

Lovat Arms Hotel on the left with petrol pumps outside Morisons Ironmongers on the right.

Today the Ironmonger shop Morisons in Beauly, is owned by Donald Fraser, and contains a unique heritage of memorabilia associated with Grant, Morison, Skinner and Riddell, plus copies of two books; (i) 'Alexander Battan Grant – his life and legacy', an authoritative account of his life, including his association with Beauly, and (ii) 'Two Highland fiddlers +2' which traces the continuous teaching connection of traditional fiddle music and composition up to the present day via a simple croft situated on the Moor of Clunes near Beauly. [Both books by this Author].

The heritage room upstairs displays some timeless items, e.g. one of Battan Grant's hand made violins, James Scott Skinners actual will, in addition to original music manuscripts, photographs, and prints from a bye gone era.

Morisons Ironmongers Beauly in 2019 (© Sinclair Gair)

Donald Morison, the son of Roderick Morison, Ironmonger, Beauly was a local fiddle player of note. He had an excellent reputation as a fine fiddler, so much so that he became assistant leader of the Highland Strathspey and Reel Society under Grant in 1903. This in turn completed a tripartite lasting friendship with the noted 'Strathspey King', James Scott Skinner whom Grant had first met in 1890.

Music for 'The Bonnie Lass o' Inverness' by Scott Skinner.

This hand-written manuscript (dated 27 June 1891) was sent to Grant by Skinner. It contains the music Skinner's composition, 'The Bonnie Lass o' Inverness', composed by Skinner. At the foot of the music Skinner has written, 'To, Sandy Grant o' Battangorm with the composer's regards'.

One of Scott Skinner's best tunes has an indirect connection with Donald Morison. On one occasion, when Scott was Donald's guest, he was taken on a drive-up Glen Strathglass to a famous and beautiful spot on the edge of the River Beauly. Sadly, this was the scene some time before of a serious road accident. A traction engine and two trucks had plunged off the road into a gorge and had killed two work men, the damage to the wild birch trees growing on the banks of the river being clearly still visible. The sadness of the event moved Scott Skinner to write the tune titled 'The Weeping Birches of Kilmorack'. Skinner later published a tune in honour of his friend titled 'Dr. Morison's Seven Thistles' – (still regularly played in a Gay Gordons reel set by Scottish dance bands to this day - including mine). Donald Fraser still recalls the time when 'giant?' thistles grew annually in the space between the two buildings at the east end of the shop when his father was still alive.

In more recent times Donald Fraser has set up a heritage display in a small room above the shop which now display's a number of items and artefact's – e.g. Skinners actual will and testament, hand-written on a small piece of paper, still hangs in a pitch pine panel room upstairs in the shop (Scott Skinner died in 1927). In relatively recent times, a downstairs room in the shop also contained a collection of disused phonograph equipment which Morison had no longer found a use for, and had superseded them with more up to date versions whilst still retaining the previous models. These unfortunately were later discarded and probably contained the only sound recordings of Battan Grant that could have provided us with a unique opportunity to hear him play.

Donald Morison was a man clearly deeply immersed in his love of Highland fiddle music, and must have greatly enjoyed the companionship of his two close friends, Grant and Skinner, when they came to visit and play tunes together.

For those with a love of Scots traditional fiddle music a trip to the Phipps Hall on Station Road where James Scot Skinner performed, is a well worth excursion. Skinner was greatly admired locally in Beauly and performed in the Phipps Institution (as then) on many occasions.

PHIPP'S INSTITUTE, BEAULY.

The Phipps Institution was built on what was then a green field site on Station Road.

The Lovat estate office building is on the right and still serves the same purpose today.

Funds to build the Hall were provided by a wealthy American businessman who annually rented the sporting rights on Beauly Castle Estate from the Lovat family. Some say that this was in recompense for an unfortunate incident on the Beauly river some time previously. Apparently two locals were caught poaching salmon from one of the river pools – the estate Gillie(s) attempted to dis-wade them from this practice by discharging a loaded shot gun at their rear ends as they departed. Unfortunately, and understandably, this caused some slight injury which eventually culminated in court action taken out by the villains seeking compensation, as a result of which some money was handed out in recompense. At a later date, in an attempt to retain good favour with the villagers, Mr Phipps generously put up the money to build the hall – something which the local people were immensely proud off, and which serves an excellent purpose today. An amusing after-tale is told about one of the complainants - seemingly flushed with his new-found wealth, he had approached his crofting neighbour with an offer to buy her croft – which she turned down. Apparently, she was overheard some-time later telling a friend that if he wanted to buy her croft he would need another shot in the arse!.

W. J. Hepburn

Phipp's Institute, Beauly

Phipps Hall plays a very valuable role in the Beauly community today, and has hosted a number of concerts by Donald Riddle's prodigy led violin group 'Blazin Fiddles'.

It is said that Donald Morison suffered very badly from insomnia and had a cellar, below the museum room where he played his violin, soundproofed, so that he could play at night without causing disturbance to his sleeping neighbours. It is also said that he was the first in the district to buy a bicycle with an electric dynamo in order to allow him to pedal about at night - thereby avoiding the pot-holes in the road. Needless to say, Donald was quite unsympathetic towards any of his staff who had slept in and arrived late for work.

He was also known to be rather eccentric. Notes from the book 'The Village of Beauly', 2001, record that at the Kilmorack Parish Council meeting held on the 16th May, 1908, they elected Donald Morison, Ironmonger, to the Beauly Ward (7 seats). It must have indeed contributed to some lively discussions having an eccentric present.

Donald Morison with glasses on, front row,

with Sandy Battan on his right-hand side

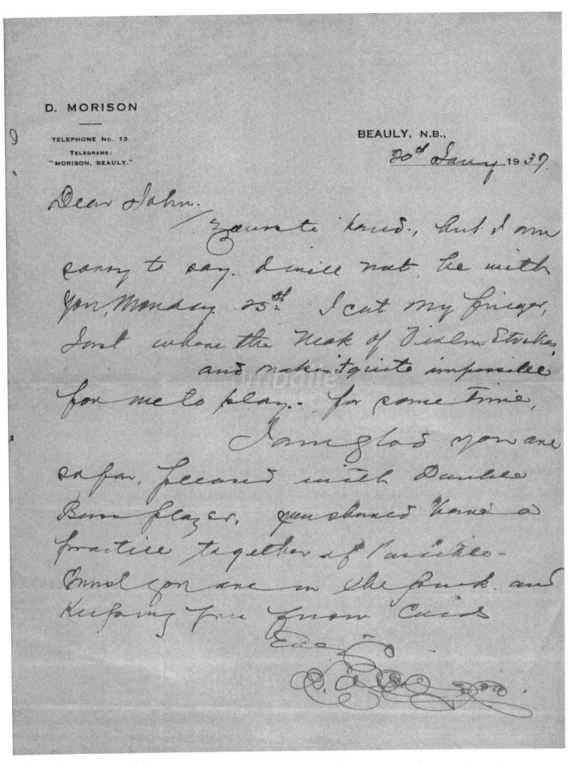

D. MORISON

TELEPHONE No. 13.
TELEGRAMS:
"MORISON, BEAULY."

BEAULY, N.B.,
20th Jany 1937

Dear John.

Yours to hand, but I am sorry to say, I will not be with you, Monday 25th. I cut my finger, just where the neck of Violin Strokes, and make it quite impossible for me to play.. for some time,

I am glad you are so far, pleased with Double Bass player, you should have a practice together of variables. And you are in the funds. and keeping free from Critics

&c

D. Morison

Letter from D. Morison, Assistant Leader, Highland Strathspey & Reel Society.

This letter dated 20 January 1937 is from the Highland branch Assistant Leader, Mr. D. Morison of Beauly, to 'John' (probably John Fraser, Secretary). In it, Mr. Morison explains he cannot attend the next concert as he has cut his finger and is unable to play.

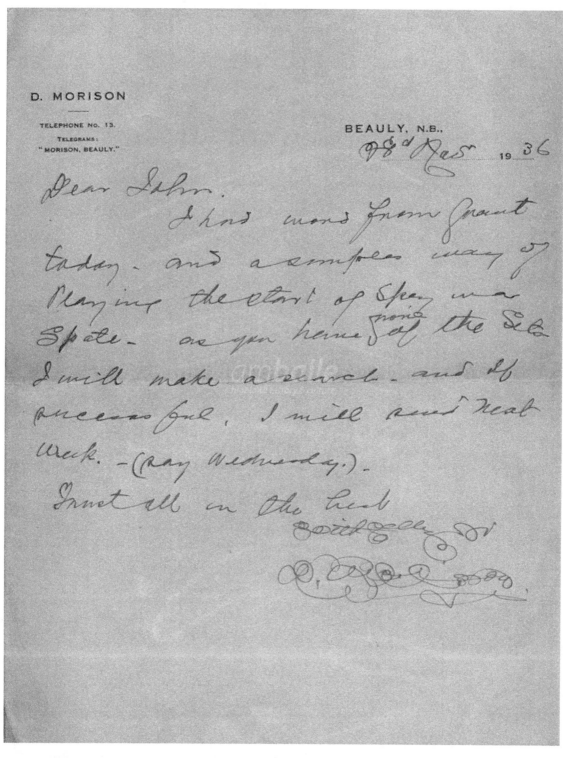

D. MORISON

TELEPHONE No. 13.
TELEGRAMS:
"MORISON, BEAULY."

BEAULY, N.B.,
28d Nov 19 36

Dear John.

I had word from Grant today - and a simpler way of playing the start of Spey in a Spate - as you have got at the Sett I will make a search - and if successful, I will send next week. - (say Wednesday.) -

Trust all in the best

Faithfully

D. Morison

Letter from D. Morison, Assistant Leader, Highland Strathspey & Reel Society.

This letter dated 28 November 1936 is from the Highland branch Assistant Leader, Mr. D. Morison of Beauly, to 'John' (probably John Fraser, Secretary). In it, Mr. Morison explains he has received, from Alexander Grant, a simpler way of playing 'Spey in a Spate', one of Scott Skinner's compositions.

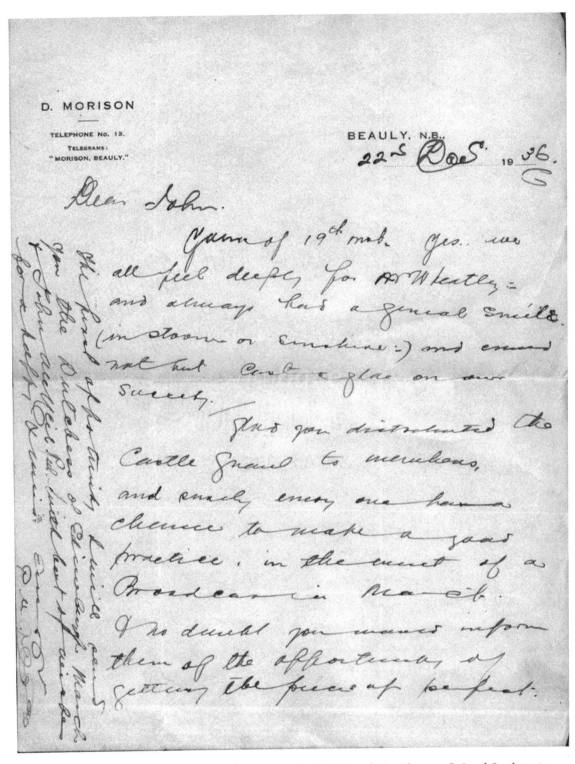

Letter from Donald Morison, Assistant Leader, Highland Strathspey & Reel Society to 'John' (probably John Fraser, Secretary)

In addition to concerts held in Inverness when Skinner was the invited guest artist, the three friends would have enjoyed many musical opportunities to play together in the down-stairs sound proofed room in Morisons Ironmongers in Beauly. Their mutual respect for one another lives on in the tribute compositions of Grant and Skinner to their enduring friendship.

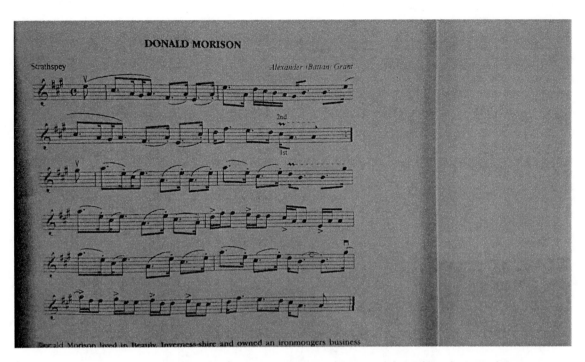

This tribute composition by Grant to his Strathspey and Reel Society assistant

leader, Donald Morison, remains to this day a popular piece

A reel, one of several, composed in honour of Grant by James Scott Skinner

The Grant collection at IMAG also holds this unique hand written version of a pipe march which Grant composed for Skinner.

Grant's original handwritten composition in honour of Skinner

This march is an important part of the highland music heritage, and is still regularly played by Inverness pipe band one hundred years (as of now), after Grant composed it.

For clarity, and ease of reading a typed manuscript version follows.

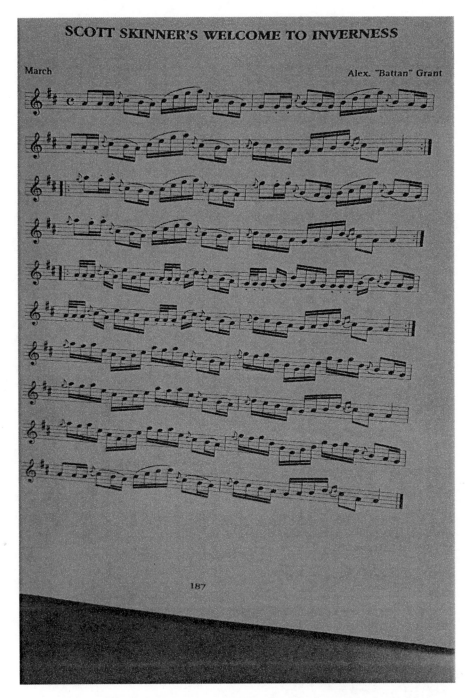

This composition by Grant was originally titled the 'King's Welcome

To Inverness' (meaning of course the Strathspey King – not the other one), and is still

played regularly by the Society and Inverness Pipe Band.

The following letter sent from Skinner to Grant dated 20th May 1915 from Carnoustie, [see 'Alexander Battan Grant' his Life and Legacy, chapter 3, by the author. (Note – the complete known correspondence from Skinner to Grant, is held by www.ambaile.org.uk). In it he expresses the wish that as he has not heard from his friend Donald Morison for some time - he hopes that all is well.

3.

When, I don't know —

You will have a call now
& again from Donald
Morison he owes me
a letter let's trust all is
well with him brave Soul

I had a letter from MacKenzie Hay
Yesterday & I learn that
Dr Cantlie's Son is on
a Submarine also
Mr Hay's Son — damnable
destruction to human beings
who never had a quarrel
the Capitalists will reap
the benefit if we win
which we must or be blotted out

The bulk of the letter is taken up with the war and its effects on friends, acquaintances, and family members. Personages specifically mentioned include Major Kenneth Macdonald of Skeabost (a Lovat Scout), Donald Morison (Assistant Leader of The Highland Strathspey and Reel Society), MacKenzie Hay (President of the Strathspey and Reel Society of London), and Mrs McHardy (wife of William McHardy, Laird of Drumblair and one of Skinner's benefactors). Skinner also mentions a forthcoming concert in Dundee in aid of war funds.

The war also had its influence on the terminology Skinner used in a later letter sent to Grant.

Glencoe, Carnoustie.
20 May 1916.

Beloved Battan,
What's yer fiddle like
a 'Zepplin'? . gie it a gweed name

· Gavin McMillan, is the yersel
a dear freen o' 'the King'

· So Jessie MacLachlan
is yne! Pity 'tis 'tis true

'One by one they rise to leave us,
They who teach us to be great'

Bless yer ain amen   J. Scott Skinner

It begins, 'What's' yer fiddle like / a Zepplin?' (Skinner published a humorous hornpipe, 'The Zeppelin' during the First World War).

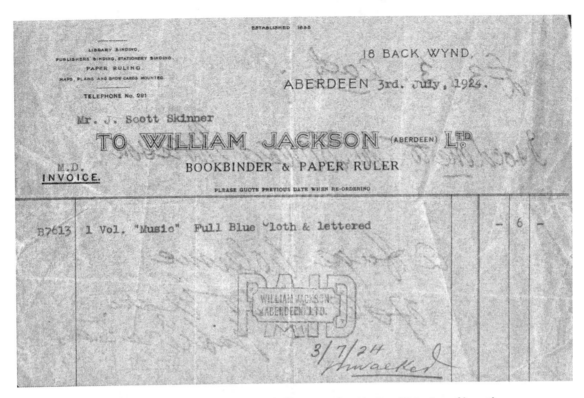

Invoice to Scott Skinner from William Jackson, Bookbinders (front).

This invoice from Aberdeen bookbinders William Jackson was sent to Grant from Skinner. It is for a bound volume of Skinner's music, priced 6 shillings. On the back is a note from Skinner which reads '£3 3s each. I sold one to Mr. Donald Morison. A Huge Volume of all my 50 years publications'.

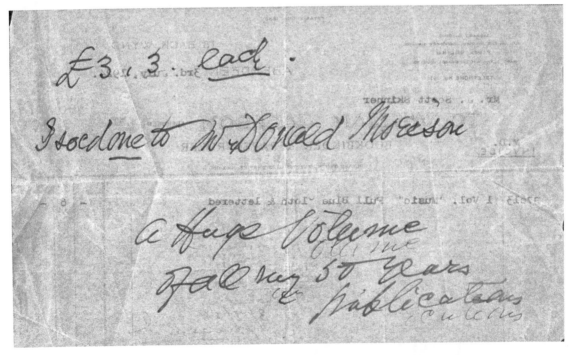

Invoice to Scott Skinner from William Jackson, Bookbinders (back).

Compositions by Skinner honouring Grant

It is not known which particular instrument Skinner was referring to here in the following composition – obviously one of the many which Grant produced. (did he intend it to have a pre-dominant bass sound?).

Strath Spey

Battans Bass Fiddle
'es Battans Bass Fiddle
It's jist the thing to fit the fleer
An' roun' aboot the middle

by J. Scott Skinner

Red hot, April 23. 1909

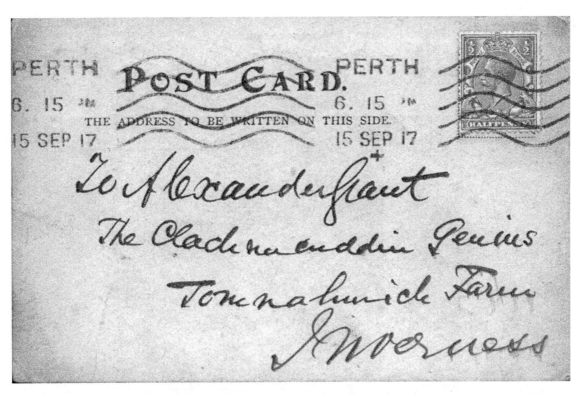

This postcard from the Salutation Hotel in Perth, 15 September 1917, was sent by Skinner to Grant, 'The Clachnacuddin Genius', at Tomnahurich Farm, Inverness – headed by a typical Skinner honorary title.

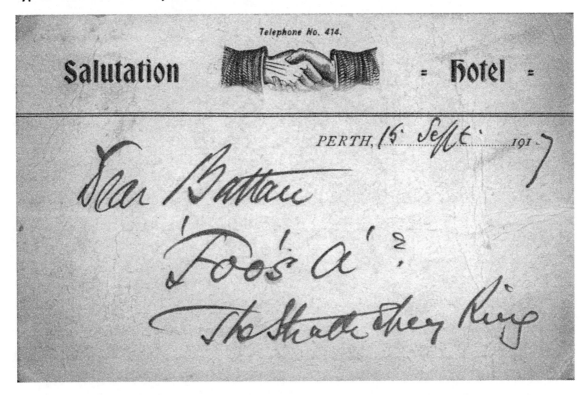

Skinner's short message to Battan enquires in his often repeated phrase 'Foo's A' – how are you? (And at other times when feeling in poor health, he quotes the aphorism 'Whom the

Gods love die young', or in more melancholy mood – 'To meet, to cheer, to know and then to part, is the sad tale of many a human heart'.

The Present Day

The following photos (taken Dec. 1919) give a general impression of the contents of the Heritage room and its treasured items which have been carefully looked after by the current owners.

Donald Fraser Holds an Original Grant Rondello now in the possession of

Grant's great grandson Michael Kerr

(© Sinclair Gair)

**Michael Kerr, Grant's great grandson, plays Donald a tune on one
of his own hand crafted fiddles.
(Scot Skinner, a frequent visitor in here, watches on from the wall.)**

(© Sinclair Gair)

Music and Memorabilia Relating to Skinner

(© Sinclair Gair)

The inscription beneath reads:

'To Donald Morison

From his friend - The Strathspey King

Signed: J Scott Skinner'

April 14th 1908

(© Sinclair Gair)

Skinner and his copious writing on a hand written pastoral composition

(© Sinclair Gair)

Grant's endearing friendship with Skinner (from 1890), was so strong that he named his first son James Scott Skinner Grant. In the following letter dated December 1905, Skinner writes to his name-sake, and concludes with the following unusual piece of advice - "Fear God and keep your bowels open"!!!

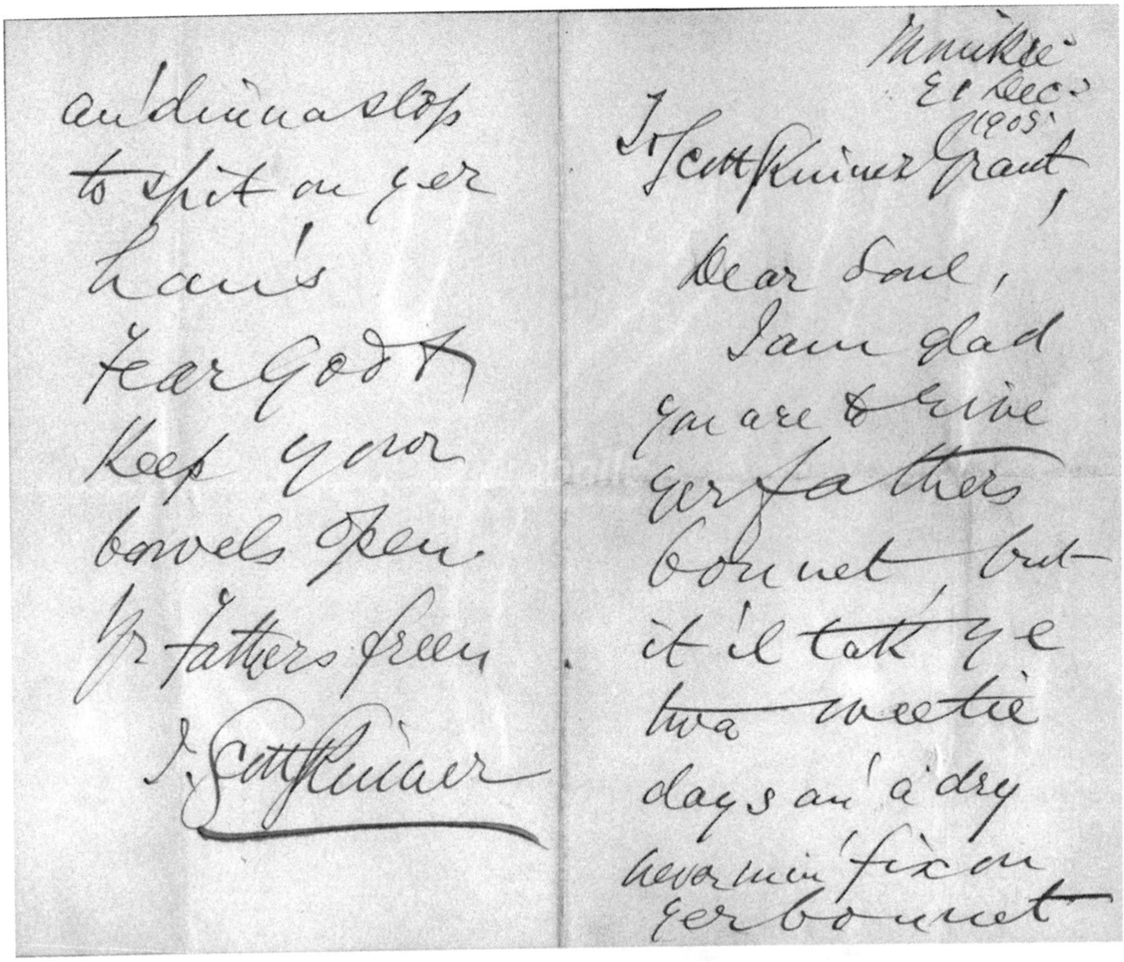

an'dinna slop
to spit on yer
han's
fear God &
keep your
bowels open.
Yr fathers freen

J Scott Skinner

Monikie
21 Dec
1905
To Scott Skinner Grant,
Dear Soul,
I am glad
you are to wire
yer fathers
bonnet, but
it il tak ye
twa weetie
days an' a dry
nevar min' fix on
yer bonnet

Letter to Grant from Skinner, Dec 1905, pages 1 & 2.

This letter dated December 1905 was sent to Grant's son, Scott Skinner Grant, by Skinner from Monikie, by Dundee. Scott was named after his father's friend.

Note to Grant from Scott Skinner, pages 1 & 2.

This note to Grant from Skinner (undated) contains lists of Scottish laments, marches, hornpipes, strathspeys and reels (many of them Skinner's own compositions). The note also contains the music for a strathspey entitled 'Scott Skinner Grant' (Alexander Grant's son).

Music for 'Glengrant' by Scott Skinner.

This is the sheet music for 'Glengrant', a strathspey composed by Scott Skinner and contained within his 'Monikie Series' (No. 2). The sheet is signed, 'To / Scott Skinner Grant / at the front / fae a man at back / 'King'. Scott Skinner Grant was one of Alexander Grant's sons, named after his father's friend.

OUR STRING BAND.

Have you all heard our famed string band,
That Mr. Grant he does command.
This fact you will understand;
I'ts the best band in our country.

Since Scott Skinner gie'd awa,
Now Mr. Grant he beats them a',
He is a credit to us all;
And we're all right proud of Sandy.

In our String Band there are many more,
Yes I believe there's quite a score;
Who can play Strathspeys and Reels galore,
But there's na ane can play like Sandy.

He can fairly make a fishing rod, a fiddle or a bow,
He can beat Stradivorius or yet Neil Gow.
I tell you now dear comrades, there are brains beneath his pow.
There's na the like of him in Bonnie Scotland.

We never can forget when up to London he did go,
The Cockney lads invited him his fishing rod to show;
They a'got flabbergasted at the line that he could throw,
For upon the Thames he beat the world's champion.

And then again dear comrades it was really grand to see,
The exhibition that he gave the king upon the Dee;
And that night the Royal family, they had salmon for their tea
And the King himself was awful proud of Sandy.

If you'r oppressed with grief or care,
Got a pain in your head or any other where;
Go down to Grant and I do declare,
He will cure you better than a doctor.

For his melodies Strathspeys and Reels,
Puts life in your heart right down to your heels;
Ten years younger one aye feels,
When listening to his music.

And Johnie Fraser you all know,
To come and help he is never slow;
His fingers he can make them go,
He can fairly play to Sandy.

The noble "Grants" of Strathspey fame,
That trusted honoured highland name;
And down from Beauly the Frasers came,
And they're both here hale and hearty.

Long may this twa our String Band lead,
Long may they help in time of need;
For they're twa right jolly chaps indeed,
And we're all proud of their music.

And may this music live for aye,
Let our band play up from June till May;
For there's nothing that will cheer like a good Strathspey
When ye get a wee down hearted.

You'll all agree with me when I say,
It fairly cheers us up when we hear Batton play;
The "Welcome", Banks, a Reel or Strathspey,
He can make us all feel young though we were ninety.

Let us all join together and wish Batton great success.
And his cronie Johnie Fraser health and happiness;
And every other member of this band in Inverness,
For they fairly do their bit to make us happy.

'Our String Band', a Poetic Tribute to Alexander Grant (Battan).

This typed manuscript entitled 'Our String Band' is a poetic tribute to Alexander Grant as Leader of the Highland Strathspey and Reel Society. Other musicians mentioned include

Scott Skinner, Stradivorious [Stradivarius], Neil Gow, and Johnie Fraser (fellow band member and society secretary).

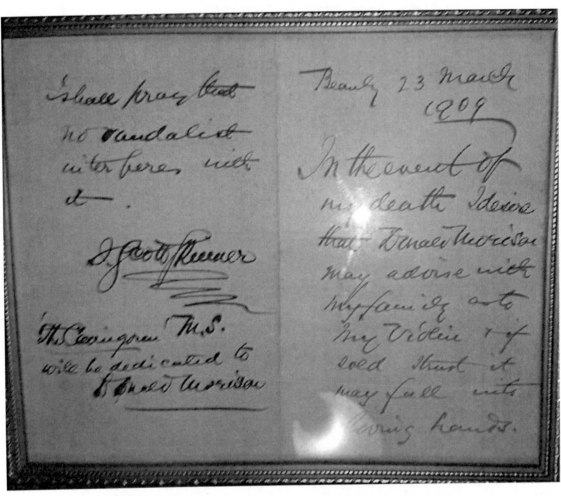

James Scott Skinners hand written 'Last Will & Testament'.

(It just happened to fall out of a handful of manuscripts and papers which Donald had picked up, and evidently had come into the possession of Donald Morison – his friend.)

(© Sinclair Gair)

A tribute to Grant from the well respected Aberdeenshire fiddler, J. Murdoch Henderson.

J. Murdoch Henderson

(Produced "Flowers of Scottish Melody")

"Battan, one of our most esteemed musical friends and well known to J.S.S. for more than half a century, was considered by the Strathspey King as an "excellent violinist".

Battan's outstanding musical gifts are reflected in the solid, good work of the Highland Strathspey and Reel Society of which he has been leader and conductor since its inception in, 1903. "

The New Highland Strathspey & Reel Society

In 1973, Donald Riddell, who had been deputy leader before the war, re-formed, and took personal charge of the Highland Strathspey and Reel Society. For the next 19 years until his death, he led the society with vigour and enthusiasm. His own fiddling talent, combined with his vast knowledge of traditional technique and his rare teaching ability, soon brought a wonderful quality and boldness to the society's playing.

Donald Riddell who re-formed the Highland Strathspey and Reel

Society in the 1970's

Many of the young pupils he taught enjoyed much success at competitions throughout Scotland and went on to make a name for themselves as professional musicians.

The re-formed Inverness Highland Strathspey and Reel Society

under Donald Riddell – note the range of age groups

Donald had an interesting method for teaching young pupils. He would write out the tune to be played -right in front of the pupil – with all bowing carefully marked out. The pupil had the written music as a guide but learnt the tune by watching and listening to Donald carefully bowing it out. The pupil was expected to learn the tune by heart and play it correctly by the next lesson – otherwise no new tune.

Like his mentor, Alexander Grant, Donald restricted the Society's repertoire to a fixed number of sets, adding to the list only occasionally. Players became very familiar with the music and knew how to play it fluently. Years later, when members of the Society meet up, they unerringly play the 'old' tunes with exactly the same bowing and vigour as when they played under Donald's command.

Quote from Duncan Chisholm – "When I joined the Society there was a membership of approximately 30 members as I remember. These people varied in age from 10 years old to people in their 70's. There was a wide variety of styles and abilities within the Society, but all were asked to play with the same bowing and in the same military style. As they played, all were watched meticulously by Donald and although never directly pointed at, were made aware somehow that all was not right if the bowing they were playing was incorrect".

A Modern Tribute to Alexander Battan Grant

Held in Inverness 77 Years

after his Death

On the 14th June 2019

June 14th 2019

ACADEMY STREET
- INVERNESS -
Townscape Heritage Project

Traditional music session and talk to celebrate the work of Alexander "Battan" Grant

A free talk sharing the stories and music of Alexander "Battan" Grant, followed by a celebratory traditional music session, has been organised by the Inverness Townscape Heritage Project at MacGregor's Bar (at the junction of Academy Street and Church Street), 5-6pm, 14th June.

As part of its ongoing bid to create a greater understanding and appreciation of the history of Inverness, Inverness Townscape Heritage Project (ITHP) is hosting a talk entitled 'Stories and Music of Alexander Battan Grant'.

In the talk, Dr Sinclair Gair will bring to life the stories and music of Alexander "Battan" Grant, who was known for his superb fiddle playing and composing, as well as the design and construction of stringed instruments. A selection of his tools and artefacts from the Inverness Museum and Art Gallery will also be on display.

Speaking ahead of the event, Dr Sinclair Gair said: "Born in 1856, Alexander Grant was a British record holding distance fly casting champion; patented inventor of a new type of fishing rod 'The Grant Vibration Rod'; violin instrument maker and inventor of a new type of violin, the 'Rondello'. Grant worked methodically on everything he did, and I look forward to sharing details of his fascinating work. I hope to bring his work to life by also playing two of his compositions on the accordion - a strathspey *'Donald Morison'* and a march *'Scott Skinners Welcome to Inverness'* - followed by a move into the modern era of west coast style traditional playing."

The celebration of Grant's work will continue with a traditional music session with Bruce MacGregor, violin, and friends.

Musician and owner of MacGregor's Bar, Bruce MacGregor, said: "We're absolutely delighted to be hosting this event for this giant of the Scottish music world. My links to Alexander Grant are through the music taught to me by Donald Riddell who was a pupil of Grant. Donald often spoke about him and taught us the tunes and the style that Grant was such a stickler for.

"We have pictures of Grant and Riddell on our Highlander's Club wall of fame. So, this just ties it all in very nicely. It'll be great to hear more about Grant from Sinclair who has done a tremendous amount of research on the man."

The event takes place 5-6pm on 14th June at MacGregor's Bar, Academy Street, Inverness and is free to attend.

About the Inverness Townscape Heritage Project (ITHP)

The Townscape Heritage Project is a grant-giving scheme that helps communities to regenerate Conservation Areas displaying particular social or economic need.

Focusing on Academy Street, the Townscape Heritage Project involves funding from the National Lottery Heritage Fund, Historic Environment Scotland (HES) via the Inverness City Heritage Trust (ICHT) and The Highland Council, contributing to a project fund, from which grants are given to local property owners, businesses and organisations to allow them to carry out high-quality repairs and historic reinstatement to properties and spaces within the defined Townscape Heritage area.

The speaker: Sinclair Gair (Author)

Bruce Macgregor plays the Strathspey, 'Donald Morison', Comp. by Grant (Some contents of Grant's workshop shown in the open case, IMAG)

The corner of Academy Street and Church Street (as it was in Grant's time - just before the 1939 War). All of the buildings shown in this photograph have now gone (except for the church spire). The first building on the left in Academy Street is now the site of MacGregors Bar as shown below.

(Courtesy of Inverness Field Club – Old Inverness in Pictures)

MacGregor's Bar taken on the evening of the tribute talk (14/06/2019)

(Forty people in attendance – house full)

(© Sinclair Gair)

Sandy Grant: His Own Brief Personal History Story

The following was taken from a hand-written account by Grant himself, found on the back of an old envelope.

I had to give up my forestry occupation and rest from manual labour for two years owing to a lacerated lung and the putting up of blood and went home to Battangorm in the Parish of Duthil. I was a bit of a fiddler and not satisfied with the fiddle I had nor others I tried. Having now the time, I started the – to me inspiring hobby of fiddle making. While pursuing my experiments and after making a number of different weights of thicknesses, I discovered what I understood to be a thread of vibration and found the fiddle to be a mere semi box with a boxy tone built on arbitrary lines and having no true scale on any part of the fingerboard. To proceed on different lines lay in obscurity [at this time] and the only thing left for me was the thread of vibration I discovered.

I was a keen angler from infancy fishing the Battangorm burns. When sound enough in health, I took a season's job as a fisherman to Sir [Michael] Arthur Bass (later Lord Burton) at Glen Quoich Forest. Going there year after year for four years in the fishing season and using my own make of rod, had the advantage and experience of seeing and using the guest's rods in comparison to my own. Some preferred their own and some mine but neither theirs nor my own provided what I felt should constitute the balance of a correct rod.

Eventually, I opened a shop in Inverness as a fishing rod and tackle maker. We had free days on the Ness every eight day and I was taking advantage of this like others and still experimenting how to make a correct rod. I got the mania for both angling and rod making which helped me in the rod and tackle business. This went on for 2 or 3 years, and scarcely a free day but I was coming home with a broken rod, not being able from an even effort to get an even result and, when forced to cast a long line, snap goes the rod. If, going out with the best rod I could make, no better result could be got, I made up my mind never to fish again unless I could make a correct rod.

After landing 2 salmon from the pool, I was fishing and casting again when snap goes the rod as usual. Two young fishing friends came along as I was leaving the pool and one of them said you are a "hell of a man". There is scarcely a free day but you are breaking your rod; if you had to pay for them, you would be more careful and satisfied with a shorter fishing line. I said: that may be so but you will never see me fishing again unless I can make a correct balanced rod. They said: we are using your rods and they are the best we ever handled. I was told [by them]: once a fisher always a fisher – and you will never make a better rod. I said: if not, that settles it – I will never fish again. The night before the free day they always came to me about the state of the water and the kind of flies to be used and always the same interrogation: was I going to fish. And always the same reply: I'm further off from making a correct rod than ever so that they need not trouble any more about me going to fish.

The evening before the fourth free day I sat down and in a moment it occurred to me: what about the thread of vibration I discovered when fiddle experimenting and would it apply to fishing rod? And no sooner thought than there a way to make it, complete in itself power for weight. In comes my two fisher friends and one of them says we need not ask any more about you going to fish. I was greatly elevated and answered as easily as I could that I was not going to fish tomorrow but all being well I would be out on the next free day.

The Tomnahurich Grants, c.1913

(Sandy at Age 57 with all his family)

Back: Willie, Annie, Jock; Middle: Sandy, Jim, Bessie

Front: Alec, Madge

Following the sale of his fishing tackle buisness in Baron Taylor Lane in 1900, Grant moved to Tomnahurich farm and started, at the age of fify, the lifestyle of an old-time farmer – a distinctly heavy occupation in those days. This would have become a way of life that was neither easy nor particularly lucrative – hence his music and fishing must have offered soothing comfort for the man.

Scott Skinner makes mention of this change in living circumstances in a letter to Grant sent from Monikie, by Dundee, dated 14th January, 1906 in which he notes "..if you have sheep, cows and acres well done...", and reproduced here:

Tomnahurich and Caledonian Canal, Inverness.

Viewed from the North, Tomnahurich farm-house is clearly visible

at the base, and towards the left-hand side of Tomnahurich Hill (Cemetery).

(Tomnahurich translates as 'the hill of the yew trees' and is also known as the 'Fairy Hill')

The farmhouse outer buildings, of U-shed formation, obscure the lower half of his house – see map below. This would have been a scene, (picture taken from what is now Kinmylies housing estate), very familiar to Grant, of the Caledonian canal and his surrounding farmland – though it is not possible to determine how much of the green fields (now housing) he actually farmed. Despite their green appearance there would likely have been a range of crops grown e.g. barley, wheat, corn, potatoes, and hay for winter feeding – e.g. as shown on the hay cart below.

The paddle steamer wending its way on the last stage of its journey up the Caladonian Canal to its destination at Muirtown Pier plied this route and may well be the Gondolier, the most famous of all the many vessels which carried passengers from Banavie, near Fort William, to Inverness, for73 years from 1866 to 1939. Freight and passenger travel by paddle steamer was the major means of transport through the Great Glen before the development of road and rail systems. This steamer would have been functioning during Grant's ownership of Tomnahurich, and he may well have used it when employed as a fisherman to Lord Burton at Glenquoich Forest, Glen Garry, in 1885, and as a gamekeeper on another estate in 1886. [the steamer ended up in 1940 being sunk as a blockship in one of the entrances to the huge naval base at Scapa Flow, Orkney].

Sandy Grant – the elderly Tomnahurich famer loading corn

sheafs onto his cart with his son

Tomnahurich Farm c.1913

(Standing: Madge, Alec & Sandy Grant)

Final image of Sandy standing outside his farm house

In the background, encroachment of 1930's housing development along what is now Bruce Gardens Road towards Tomnahurich farmhouse. The spire of St Stephens church – the old High Church, is clearly visible, top left. Further housing development in the mid 1950's led to the obliteration of the farm.

Letter from Alexander Grant to his nephew:

Inverness

12.12.35

My Dear Nephew,

You are a credit to all belonging to you and markedly to your Battangorm forefathers of whom you are a true descendant. But damit I can't get out of the multifarious position I am placed in and regret delay in answering your grand and eloquent letter of 27th July last. But

103

my dear William it's not for the want of thinking about you and your kind and natural disposition.

Your token of a carved ivory fisherman with rod in hand is a present that will go down the ages! It is a marvellous work of art, one friend on seeing it remarked, "At last Battan's god's arrived!". Yes I replied, God was made by man and not man made by god!... You will be glad to hear – and not before time – it (my god) arrived safely. Your letter is remarkable in various ways, its terseness in elucidating the subject of rods, fishing, adverts and eggs for hatching from Blagdon Lake. This loch "Jock Scott" fishes year after year and kills trout up to 6 lb weight so that the spawn from it will serve you very well. Out there and receiving xxxxx from such a distance.

Your referring to Blagdon Lake and spawn from it induced me to send "Jock Scott" your letter. He published another book since you left for Hong Kong, "Greased Line Fishing for Salmon". Herewith his letter on sending me above book. He was very pleased to have got a reading of your letter which he returned and thoroughly agreed with you. He was north again this year seeing me. Before coming up here he was approached by a London Publisher to write a book comprising fishing done throughout the world wherever fishing is done – biggest bags on different waters, heaviest fish, longest recorded fly casting, rods and their principles and also the longest cast with fly in killing salmon. He wanted and walked to see the spot where I hooked and killed the salmon with 47 yards of line.

We all got a shock on hearing of your Uncle Willie's sudden death. I was put to a deal of trouble about it, but now off my hands having to employ a solicitor to certify deeds or other writings. He didn't expect such a sudden end and left his affairs in rather a mixed state, but one good thing his agent in W.A. knew him and probably most of his transactions for 30 years. Most of the letters received or copies were sent by Annie to your mother, who had written to you. A number of his relations and friends took shares in one of the mines he controlled, myself included and though we wished to get our shares returned at face value, it would be at a loss owing to the depreciation of the pound.

Now about the new fiddle. I'm afraid if not left from outside interference in which I'm involved and increasingly more than ever, as my nerves and energy are dwindling I may share the fate of your Uncle William and writing the great bugbear which I must elude. However, you will be glad to know I have one fiddle so far completed in detail with a resonance power and truth that it's tone should convince the most sceptical. But before proceeding with it alone, I must accompany it with a cello which can be more perfectly made or balanced (but a very stressful undertaking for me) owing to no counteractions as in the small instrument for holding under the chin. It will take celloist to their knees and never again touch their empty spurious tinpot noise boxes again.

I am writing this scribble on my knees sitting at the sooty fire in my recess where the remnants of articles made and unmade are jumbled together which you can hardly visualise!

With love to Mary and family – well and happy may they be, but don't forget a large (amount?) of my own best wishes on behalf of your noble self.

Your affectionate Uncle

Sandy.

I hope to be able to keep fit and see you all before I go.

Sandy suffered from ailments all his life. Of those we know about: 1875, a burst vein in his lung; 1908, scrotal rupture (left side), cured by a truss; 1935s, severe inflammation of the lower bowel; and, finally, chronic anaemia preceding death as a consequence of atrial fibrillation.

On 6th July 1942 Alexander Battan Grant, aged 86, passed away at the Northern Infirmary – a short walking distance from Tomnahurich farm. His wife Betsy passed on a short time later on the 2nd February 1943, age 76.

Alexander Battan Grant lies buried in Tomnahurich Cemetry, about 500 yards from the farm in which he lived for 36 years. His wife Betsy Kennedy lies with him in a four layer plot with the names of five of his six children on the grave stone. His daughter Marjory's name was added to the gravestone on her interment on 07/07/99. His son John Kennedy Grant is interred in Dores Churchyard.

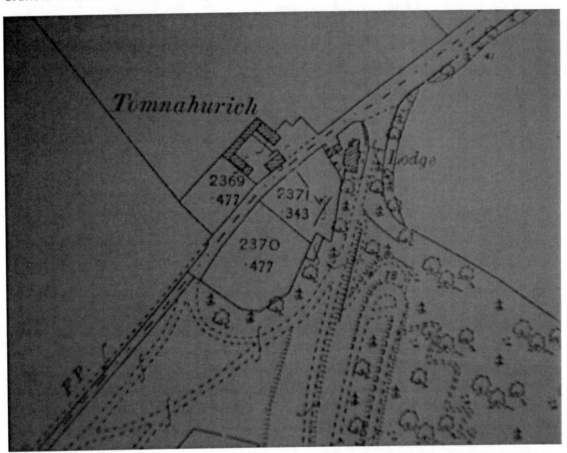

Tomnahurich Farm – showing the outline of the farm house and traditionally U-shaped

outer buildings arrangement.

(Lat: 57Deg 28Min 14" N, Long: 004Deg 14Min 37" W.)

Surveyed in 1866 & 67

Now the location of modern housing in Bruce Gardens

The Cemetery sits on and around Tomnahurich Hill (bottom right-hand corner) which one see when crossing the canal bridge going north on the A82 at the outskirts of Inverness. Grant's grave, together with those of his family, is to the right-hand side, and just below the right walkway shown above.

A Lasting Tribute

In life, Grant was described as being a wiry, slightly-built man, with finely-cut, weather-beaten features and penetrating blue-grey eyes, all surmounted by a shock of thick, tawny hair. To those who knew him he is described as a man possessed of an energy peculiar to himself, which he was able to transmit – and transmit he did, because here, seventy eight years (in 2020) after his death, and one hundred and sixty four years after his birth, people such as myself find great interest in the man, and a desire to keep his memory alive and known to the general public in oder to celebrate his achievements and contribution to Highland cultural life.

His Motto and Driving Force in Life:

"Either a thing is right or it isn't, and if it isn't, it's not worth troubling about". Similarly, "Why" he said, "take any trouble at all unless you are going to take enough? An imperfect job is no use to anyone".

Chronological Time Line:

ALEXANDER GRANT (Sandy Battan)   Rev 5, 09-05-91

1856 Born 2 Sept at Battangorm croft, CarrBridge. Battan-gorm means clump/thicket of
     blue.

1861 Census (8 Apr): living at Battangorm (age 4).
     : Left school (which overlooked Battangorm croft), (age 8).
     : Supposedly refused fiddle lessons from a neighbour (the school teacher?) because
     he didn't like the tone of his fiddle.
     :Herdsman and ploughman at Battangorm. (With no fences in those days, herding
     was necessary to keep the cattle off the crops.), (age 8/14).

1870/71 12 months as a hill shepherd at Cromdale.

1871 Census (3 April): reports Alex living at Battangorm (age 14).

1871 Apprentice draper in Wales for 2-1/2 years (age 15/17).

1874 Went to Cullen to learn forestry but later gave up due to ill health (burst blood vessel

     in lungs). (age 18).

1876 Started 2 years enforced idleness under medical stricture. (age 20).

1878/80 Started a grocer/butcher shop in Carrbridge.
     : After 18 months, he moved to Strathdearn where shop keeping offered better
     prospects. (age 22).

1881 Census (4 Apr): grocer at Garbole, Dalarossie, Upper Findhorn with brother
     Charles. Also does hair dressing. (age 24).

1882 Romance with Catherine McBain, farmer's daughter, Corrievorrie, Dalarossie.

1883 Daughter (illegitimate) Mary McBain born 20 March at Morile, Tomatin. (age 26).

1884 Daughter Mary baptised at Moy 6th January. Sandy was present but no evidence that
     Catherine McBain was. About this time, Mary was handed over for care to Sandy's
     Mother in Battangorm. Also, about this time, Sandy returns to Carrbridge where he
     starts large scale fly making but without, it seems, managing to make a sufficient
     living off it. (age 27).

1885 Takes a season as a fisherman to Lord Burton at Glenquoich Forest (up the river Garry,
     West of the Great Glen), (age 28).
     Catherine McBain, whom Sandy was thwarted from marrying, accepts her father's
     choice, Alex Tulloch, a worker on the Corrievorrie farm.

1886 Made a fiddle (the first?). His interest in the technicalities of the violin date from his
time in Strathdearn.

1886 Takes another season at Glenquoich. Later takes a position, for a short while, as a gamekeeper on another estate.

1887 Announces (24 May) move from C. Bridge to Inverness and start a shop in Glenalbyn Building, Young St, as a fishing tackle maker. Capital shortage compels him to look for extra income so he adds hairdressing to the business and hires a barber. (age 30).

1887 Further to help income, Sandy takes another season at Glenquoich. He catches a 55 lb salmon on the river Garry in September, at the outlet to Loch Quoich. (age 31).

1887/88 Discharges the barber and does the hairdressing himself as well as make fishing tackle. Leaves Young Street to take up premises at 7 Baron Taylor' Lane, now Street.

1890 Befriends Scott Skinner who admires his bowing technique. (age 33/34).

1891 Marries 29 Jan, Edinburgh, Elizabeth (Bessie) Kennedy. Address given as Baron Taylors Lane, Inverness; occupation: fishing tackle maker. (age 34).

1891 Son James Scott Skinner born 11 Nov at 4 Ardross Place, Inverness. Occupation: fishing tackle maker. (age 35).

1892 Father dies 18 Feb at Battangorm.

1892 Made guitar shaped fiddle ("No 1 Battangorm"). At this time he is putting his discoveries on the acoustic properties of wood to practical use in both violins and fishing rods.

1892 First mention in a sporting paper of the Vibration Rod (Rod & Gun Sept 3rd). This was probably due to R H Carballis of Moniack castle, a JP in Inverness, who had good contacts in the fishing world. He strongly supported Sandy in the disputes later in the 90's over casting competitions.

1893 First mention on the 7th April, 1893, in Land and Water, of the use of fall-down rings on the rod. (age 36).

1893 Daughter Ann born 27 April at 4 Ardross Place. Occupation: fishing tackle maker.

1894 Applies 28 May for patent (spliced joint for fishing rod). Patent No 10,385 of 1894 (handled by Johnsons Patent Office, Glasgow). (age 37).

1895 Son John Kennedy born 16 Feb at 4 Ardross Place. Occupation: fishing tackle maker. (age 38).

1895 Splice patent accepted 4 May. (age 40).

1896 Son, William Rose, born 6th Nov. at Ardross Place

1896 Demonstrates fly casting, Dec 10, 11, 12, to select fishing audience at Kingston-on-Thames. Opposite the Sun Hotel. Editors of "The Field", "The Fishing Gazette", "Rod and Gun", and "Land and Water" and other notables (including R H Corballis).

1899 Daughter Marjory born 7 Jul at Rowan Bank, Ballifeary Rd. (age 42).

1900 Sale of patent rights of the vibration rod to Charles Playfair, Aberdeen, for £100 plus %10 royalty per rod for 10 years. Rods to be numbered consecutively from 1. (age 45/46).

1900 Approx. date for sale of business in Baron Taylors Lane (fishing tackle maker, tin/coppersmith, hairdresser).

1901 Brother David, pipe major of the Cameron Highlanders, dies in S. Africa.

1902 Son Alexander born 26 Nov at Ballifeary Rd. (age 48).

1903 Daughter Mary marries 10 Apr at Battangorm from 4 Hill St, Inverness. Sandy's occupation given as hairdresser.

1903 Founds Highland Strathspey and Reel Society and leads it for the rest of his lifetime. (age 48).

1906 Moves to Tomnahurich farm, Inverness.

1916 Mother dies 5 Oct at Dalnansyde cottage, Carr Bridge (daughter Mary's house).

1924 Publishes "Scott Skinner's Welcome to Inverness".

1927 Scott Skinner dies.

1934 or 35 Radio broadcast of Highland Strathspey and Reel Society.

1942 Dies 6 July, aged 85.

1943 Wife Bessie dies 2 Feb, age 76.

Date unknown: caught 8 lb salmon on Ness at distance of approx. 47 yards.

A local poet, Bernard George Hoare, wrote the following lines in Grant's memory:

Master of violins and of the bow

That sweeps the strings to tuneful melody,

Player of lively airs and tunes that be

The genius of your native Strath's outflow,

With kindred genius nature did bestow

On you the finer sense of music's round

And perfect tone; the laws of sound

Enthralled you, as her child to trace and know.

Craftsman and builder of a truer tone

Than even the violin now can, mastered charm;

Who seeks for perfect finds it not alone,

Since in the seeking also lies the form.

You are the silent poet, tuning all the strings

To perfect interval, where false still rings.

From Peoples Journal
11th July 1942

Musician And Inventor

Death Of Notable Highlander

LOVERS of Highland music not only in this country but abroad will mourn the death of Mr Alexander Grant, Tomnahurich Farm, Inverness, for, a brilliant fiddler, he was one of the greatest exponents of this type of music since that other noted player, Scott Skinner.

Mr Grant, who died in the Royal Northern Infirmary on Monday after a lingering illness, devoted most part of his life to the propagation of the characteristic music of the Highlands, marches, strathspeys, and reels.

Born at Battan Gorm, near Carr Bridge, 86 years ago, Mr Grant began at the early age of 10 what turned out to be a truly remarkably brilliant career as a violinist. Even then he showed a keen sense of the true quality of music, for it is recalled by his friends that when his father sent him to a neighbour to learn to play he refused to go again because the tone of the teacher's fiddle was bad.

The Master Touch.

Principally by self-tuition Mr Grant gradually acquired the master touch, and he became such a brilliant player that he was generally regarded as being the "Scott Skinner of the Highlands."

Mr Grant had a varied and interesting career. After leaving school he was in turn a ploughman, shepherd, draper, forester, grocer, butcher, gamekeeper, fisherman, and fishing tackle merchant in Inverness.

He became tenant of Tomnahurich Farm about 40 years ago, and it was from that time that he really began to develop his very great interest in Highland music.

He accomplished much good work as leader of the Highland Strathspey and Reel Society. It was with the aim of improving the playing of marches, strathspeys, and reels that he helped to form this society some 40 years ago, and he gave it his inspired leadership from its inception until a short time ago.

As leader of the society, Mr Grant was extremely popular, not only with members but with the public. The latter delighted to see the veteran wielding the baton, and gave him a rousing reception, particularly at the time-honoured wool fair concerts given by the society round about this period of the year.

Born Genius.

"Battan," the name by which he was known to all his friends, composed several pieces of Highland music, including the march, "Scott Skinner's Welcome," and the strathspey and reel, "Donald Morison," the last-mentioned being a musical tribute to one of his oldest friends.

He was recognised by many as being a born genius with an inventive trait. He made several types of fiddles and for many years, up until his last illness, he was engaged on constructing a violin based on the vibration principle.

He claimed that this violin, which was unlike in design any other type, would, when completed, produce a tone so rich in quality and expression that it would resemble as near as possible the human voice. Unfortunately, Mr Grant did not succeed in his ambition to complete this unique violin.

Perhaps his most interesting invention was that of the Grant vibration fishing rod, which was regarded as being one of the best rods ever constructed. This invention created considerable interest amongst anglers, and Mr Grant was challenged twice to show its capabilities. Its worth was fully proved when Mr Grant, before a large crowd of anglers on the Thames, set up a record cast of 56 yards with a 21-foot rod.

Later from a boat on the River Ness he cast a distance of 65 yards with a 21-foot rod and 61 yards with an 18-foot rod.

The death of this interesting personality marks the passing of one who was popular with all who had the pleasure of his acquaintance.

He is survived by Mrs Grant and a grown-up family of four sons and two daughters.

This tribute to Alexander Grant, 'Musician and Inventor', is from the 'People's Journal', 11th July, 1942. The 'People's Journal' was one of many popular weekly papers which appeared in Scotland following the repeal of the Stamp Duties in the 1850s. From its inception in Dundee in 1858, it quickly grew into thirteen editions covering Scotland's major cities, towns and regions.

GIFTED VIOLINIST AND ANGLER

Late Mr Alexander Grant

One of the most remarkable and outstanding personalities in the North, Mr Alexander Grant, of Tomnahurich Farm, Inverness, passed away peacefully on Monday in his 87th year.

Mr Grant was a violinist of repute and was famous for his splendid rendering of Strathspeys and reels in the traditional Highland style. The late Mr Scott Skinner acknowledged that Mr Grant excelled him in bowing as well as in the playing of the older Scotch airs. To him Scott Skinner composed and published a reel named "Sandy Grant's reel." He was the leader of Inverness Strathspey and Reel Society from its inception.

Mr Grant was also an expert angler, and held the record for long line casting not only on the Ness but on the Thames.

A native of Strathspey, he, when a young man became head fisherman to the late Rt. Hon Lord Burton, lessee of the famous deerforest of Glenquoich, where he met many of the angling sportsmen of that day; to mention but two, Lord Randolph Churchill father of the present Premier, and Joe Chamberlain father of the late Premier, Neville Chamberlain.

In later years he opened up a combined hairdressing and fishing tackle maker's establishment in Inverness. He made violins on the model of the Cremona as a hobby. In order to do this he took up the study of sound-vibration which he mastered to a wonderful degree. The nature of the varnish with which the makers of the "Stradivarius and the Cremona" violins were coated was more or less unknown to modern violin makers. Mr Grant got busy, and if he came short of discovering the secret, he nevertheless succeeded in making varnish which was equally effective in coating the violin without in any way, (unlike the spirit varnish) affecting the tone of the instrument.

When applying his knowledge of sound vibration to the making of his violins it occurred to him that it would be possible to make a fishing rod in such manner as to ensure an uninterrupted flow of vibration along the fibre of the rod from butt to point and thus make the rod more pliant.

Famous Fishing Rod

In this he succeeded and turned out the best and most famous rod that was ever placed on the market. He ultimately secured a patent for it, and later sold the right to Playfair, Fishing Tackle makers, Aberdeen.

Soon the fame of the "Grant Vibration Rod" spread far and wide. This was naturally the cause of some resentment by many other good makers of rods, and in a short time all the leading sporting papers throughout England and Scotland were aflame with bitter controversy relative to the merits and demerits of the rod's casting capacity. In the end a challenge to a competition was issued to Mr Grant, and his supporters. The challenge was readily accepted and Mr Grant went to London, and in the presence of the best anglers and tackle-makers of that day, proved the superior casting capacity of his rod on the Thames without difficulty.

Within recent years, Mr Grant, not wholly satisfied that the tone produced by the violin in its present form was what it might be, made one himself on the most unorthodox lines. His view was to conserve the sound-vibration which in the case of the present model, he thought was dissipated by the "S" sound-holes. Whether he attained this end must needs be left for the expert to say, but that he produced a violin of the rarest beauty of tone, both sweet and mellow, cannot be gainsaid. The construction of it was kept secret from all but a few of his more intimate friends as he had intended to secure a patent for it. It is to be hoped that some day the patent will be secured and the new violin will become as famous as the "Vibration Rod."

A more kindly or unassuming person could not well be met with than Mr Alexander Grant. Many friends throughout the Highlands will regret his passing while this mention of his name must bring to their memories the rich feast of Highland music with which he entertained them at Woolfair Concerts of other days in Inverness.

J.T.H.

This tribute to Alexander Grant, 'Gifted Violinist and Angler', is from 'The Football Times', 11th July 1942.

Alexander Battan Grant – His Historical Archive

Sandy Grant (1890 ?)

Family photograph with Grant (2nd left), and presumeably – his wife

Betsy (centre), two of his 4 sons, and his two daughters, Ann and Marjory.

At home with family – Grant 2nd right with his wife Betsy on his right hand side.

Grant on the right with two friends

(probably taken at the same time as the studio portrait)

Grant with his eldest son James

Alexander Grant (1856 - 1942) was a native of Battangorm, Carrbridge, which gave rise to his familiar name - 'Battan'. As a boy he was exposed to what were to become his two great passions - fiddling and fishing. He went on to excel in both areas; as an angler by inventing his own unique fishing rod known as the 'Grant Vibration Rod', and as a fiddler by leading the Highland Strathspey and Reel Society for almost forty years and by becoming an expert in fiddle making techniques. He also invented a unique disc-shaped violin known as a 'Rondello'. An example of

Grant's fishing rod, fiddle and Rondello can be seen at Inverness Museum and Art Gallery (IMAG).

This photograph shows an elderly Alexander Grant (centre) at home with his daughter and friends, one of whom is holding a Grant 'Vibration' fishing rod.

Alexander Grant (1856 - 1942) - as a boy he was exposed to what were to become his two great passions - fiddling and fishing. He went on to excel in both areas; as an angler by inventing his own unique fishing rod known as the 'Grant Vibration Rod', and as a fiddler by leading the Highland Strathspey and Reel Society (1903 ~ 1942), for almost forty years and by becoming an expert in fiddle making techniques.

In May 1887 Grant moved his fishing rod and tackle business from Carrbridge to Inverness, initially at Glenalbyn Buildings, Young Street. He later moved to premises at 7 Baron Taylor's Lane. This photograph shows Grant's business premises in Baron Taylor's Lane which incorporated a tin and coppersmith, a haircutting and shaving saloon, and the fishing rod and tackle business. The gentleman standing outside the front door (centre) may be Mr. Grant in his earlier years.

A street scene in Inverness that would have been familiar to Grant. The 16th or 17th century prophet, the Brahan Seer, predicted the coming of the Caledonian Canal - "full-rigged ships will be seen sailing eastward and westward by the back of Tomnahurich". The area was also the scene of an annual horse race from the 17th century. (However, the Brahan Seer lived in dangerous times with the domination by the church and the cult of witch craft practised at the time. Following one prediction too many he was burned to death at the stake by the Mackenzies as a witch - indeed there is some doubt if he actually existed).

The Scottish Clans' Association

(of LONDON).

Association's Head Quarters:
ROYAL SCOTTISH CORPORATION HALL,
Fleet Street, E.C.
(Entrance, Crane Court.)

Chief.
Dr. W. AITKIN MAC LEOD.

Hon. President.
Gen. Sir HECTOR A. MACDONALD, K.C.B.,
D.S.O., A.D.C.

President.
DONALD N. NICOL, Esq., M.P.

Vice-Presidents.
Sir ROBERT B. FINLAY, K.C., M.P., Attorney-General.
Sir WILLIAM JOHNSTON, Bart.
ROBERT CAMERON, Esq., M.P.
JAMES MEAD SUTHERLAND, Esq.
A. C. MACKENZIE, Esq.
JAMES WATSON, Esq.   JAMES BUCHANAN, Esq.
JOHN ROEBUCK, Esq.   GEORGE ROSS, Esq.
GILMOUR ORR, Esq.   Lieut. NEIL MACKAY.
Lieut. E. S. GRAHAM, R.G.A.

Hon. Auditor:
Mr. ANGUS N. SCOTT, C.A.,
18, Ironmonger Lane, E.C.

Bankers—
Messrs. CHILD & Co.,
1, Fleet Street, E.C.

Hon. Treasurer:
GEO. C. WALLACE,
227, Regent Street, W.

Hon. Secretary:
WILLIAM MACKENZIE FRASER,
26, Portland Road,
Holland Park, W.

Hon. Assistant Secretary:
JOHN MAC INTYRE MASSON,
16. Rutland Park Mansions,
Willesden Green, N.W.

PATRONS.

His Grace the Duke of Richmond and Gordon, K.G., P.C.
His Grace the Duke of Hamilton.
His Grace the Duke of Montrose, K.T.
His Grace the Duke of Buccleuch & Queensberry, K.G., K.T.
His Grace the Duke of Argyll, K.T., G.C.M.G., P.C.
The Most Hon. the Marquess of Huntly, P.C.
The Most Hon. the Marquess of Breadalbane, K.G., P.C.
The Right Hon. the Earl of Haddington.
The Rt. Hon. the Earl of Kinnoull.

The Rt. Hon. the Earl of Dundonald, C.B., M.V.O
The Rt. Hon. Earl of Kintore, G.C.M.G., P.C.
The Rt. Hon. Lord Abinger.
The Rt. Hon. Lord Stratheden and Campbell.
The Rt. Hon. Lord Blythswood.
The Rt. Hon. Lord Kinnaird.
The Rt. Hon. A. J. Balfour, M.P., P.C.
The Rt. Hon. Lord Sinclair.
The Hon. Claude George Hay, M.P.
Sir Andrew N. Agnew, Bart., M.P.
Sir Lewis MacIver, Bart., M.P.
Sir George MacPherson Grant, Bart., of Ballindalloch.

Sir Alexander Keith Fraser, Bart.
Sir A. C. MacKenzie, Mus.Doc.
General Sir Ian Hamilton, K.C.B., D.S.O.
The Ven. Wm. MacDonald Sinclair, Archdeacon of Lond.
A. Bignold, Esq., M.P.
Colonel J. M. Denny, M.P.
Michael Hugh Shaw Stewart, Esq., M.P.
A. Ritchie, Esq., J.P., C.C.
G. N. Forbes, Esq.
W. D. MacKenzie, Esq., of Farr.

SCOTTISH CLANS' STRING & PIPE BAND.
Particulars of Practice, etc., may be obtained from the Hon. Secretaries.

SCOTTISH CLANS' LITERARY SOCIETY.
Meetings on alternate Wednesdays of every month from October to March, inclusive.

SCOTTISH CLANS' SHINTY CLUB.
Particulars of practice, etc., may be obtained from the Hon. Secretaries.

2nd August 1902.

Dear Mr Grant,

I really don't know what you will be thinking about me not answering your kind letter long ere this; I have been up to my eyes in work ever since you left. Russell and myself have many a laugh over your visit. I think that old nag going to the Station on Sunday night put the finishing tip to things.

No, don't you will be thinking it very strange not receiving your cheque yet. I only received it yesterday and have send it to the Secretary to be signed. I will have it back tomorrow and will send it on to you. It is made out for £6 "10. your letter

Letter to Grant from William Fraser, 2 Aug 1902, page 1.

keep the lot and I will square things up when I go
north, I expect to be in Inverness about the 20th
of this month.

I had a letter from my mother; herself and my
Father were delighted with your visit

Neil and his wife wishes to be kindly remembered
to you. Thanks very much for the papers you sent
me. I understand A.C. Mackenzie and his young
wife are in Inverness just now. He will likely
give you a call

This is a holiday in London but as I had
so many things to do one way and another I
did not go away. The weather here is very cold
and wet — not a bit like the beginning of August.

I am enclosing you a copy of the London Scotsman
with an account of the Concert.

Have you the Principle Russell and I have many
a chat over it.

I will send you a few lines enclosed with
the Cheque tomorrow

With kind regards.

Believe me.

Yours Sincerely

William Mackenzie Fraser

Letter to Grant from William Fraser, 2 Aug 1902, page 2.

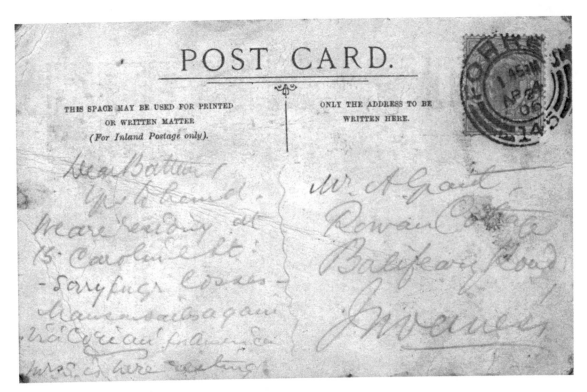

Postcard to Grant from Skinner, 24 April 1906.

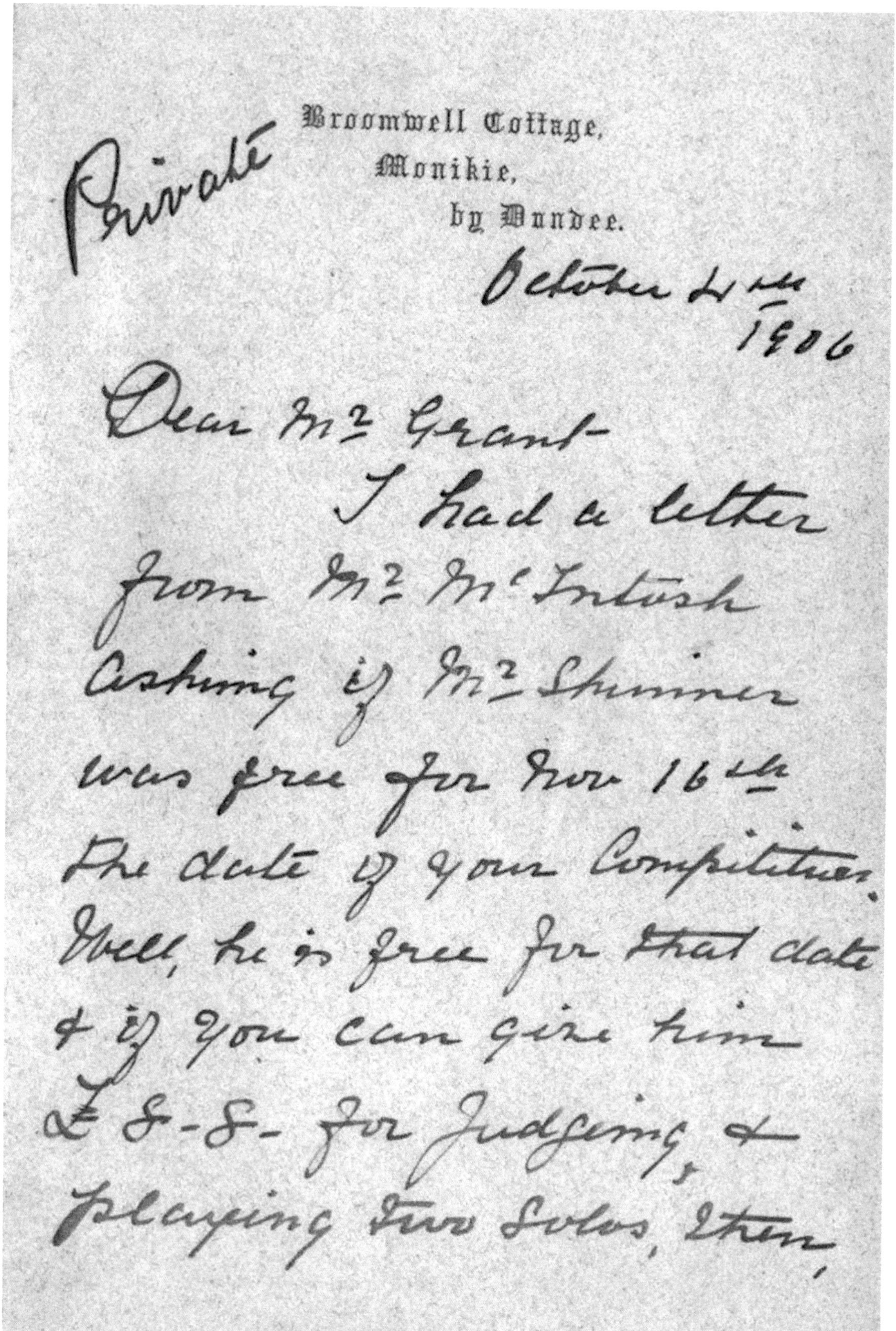

Private   Broomwell Cottage,
                      Monikie,
                   by Dundee.

                           October 4th
                              1906

Dear Mr Grant —
            I had a letter
from Mrs McIntosh
asking if Mr Skinner
was free for Nov 16th
the date of your Competition.
Well, he is free for that date
& if you can give him
£8-8- for Judging, &
playing two Solos, then,

Letter to Grant from Skinner's wife.

123

he can come, but not
for less money. Every
Committee seems to think
he should practically give
his services. These people
do not consider his age,
& that he has his living
to make. I am speaking
to you as a friend, which
I have proved you to be.
My husband has been to
Orkney & Shetland for

a fortnight with an aberdeen
Coy & is now in London
making more records on
the phonograph, He was
sent for specially, the Coy
defraying all expenses
& paying him £10 – a day
for three days.

I have been laid to one
side again, but feel better
today. Manson has been at
home since June doing nothing
& I have never in the ten
years ~~seen~~ I have known
them seen a copper coin of

Letter to Grant from Skinner's wife, 4 Oct 1906, pages 2 & 3.

his money! All this has
told on my health until
it is utterly broken down.
I trust you are all well
& with warmest regards

Believe me

Yours Sincerely
G. May Kirk-Skinner

Letter to Grant from Skinner's wife, 4 Oct 1906, page 4.

Telegrams: ABBEY, FORT AUGUSTUS.
Telephone: FORT-AUGUSTUS No. 4.
Rail Via SPEAN BRIDGE.

THE ABBEY,
FORT-AUGUSTUS.
SCOTLAND.

Feb 12th 1928

Dear Mr Grant

I hope you got back to Inverness yesterday morning, if not Friday night, quite safely & with the minimum of discomfort.

Will you please, on the first oppor-tunity that presents itself, convey to all your musical accomplices my most heartfelt thanks & the thanks of all of us present at the Concert for your very delightful & inspiriting — & I may say "inspiring — music & presence at that Concert which made it so great a success:

It will be a long time before we shall leave off talking about that music. We expected much & received more!

To yourself especially I would give my warmest thanks. It was most

Letter to Grant from Ronald Alexander, 12 Feb 1928, page 1.

126

speaking of you to come on you did on
such a height & after dark a disturb-
-aging misadventure. I still have
the suspicion that you flew over
Loch Tch with your violin tucked
under a wing!

The Rev A.L. Sarly. Elwes greatly
hopes to meet you & your Strathspeys
band at the Town Hall next Friday
on the occasion of the Scouts' Concert.
I greatly, too, want you to hear
our Boys' Orchestra of which we are
rather proud. A very few years ago it
had no existence. But I wish you
could teach them to add Strathspeys
to their other beautiful items!

Strathspeys, to my mind, beside their
beautiful music, are the Folk Music
of a great race & charged with the
spirit of the Highland Race. Like
the Gaelic Songs they are incomparable.
With very good wish to you & John Fraser
& all of the Society, believe me
Yours very heartily, Ronald Alexander

Letter to Grant from Ronald Alexander, 12 Feb 1928, page 2.

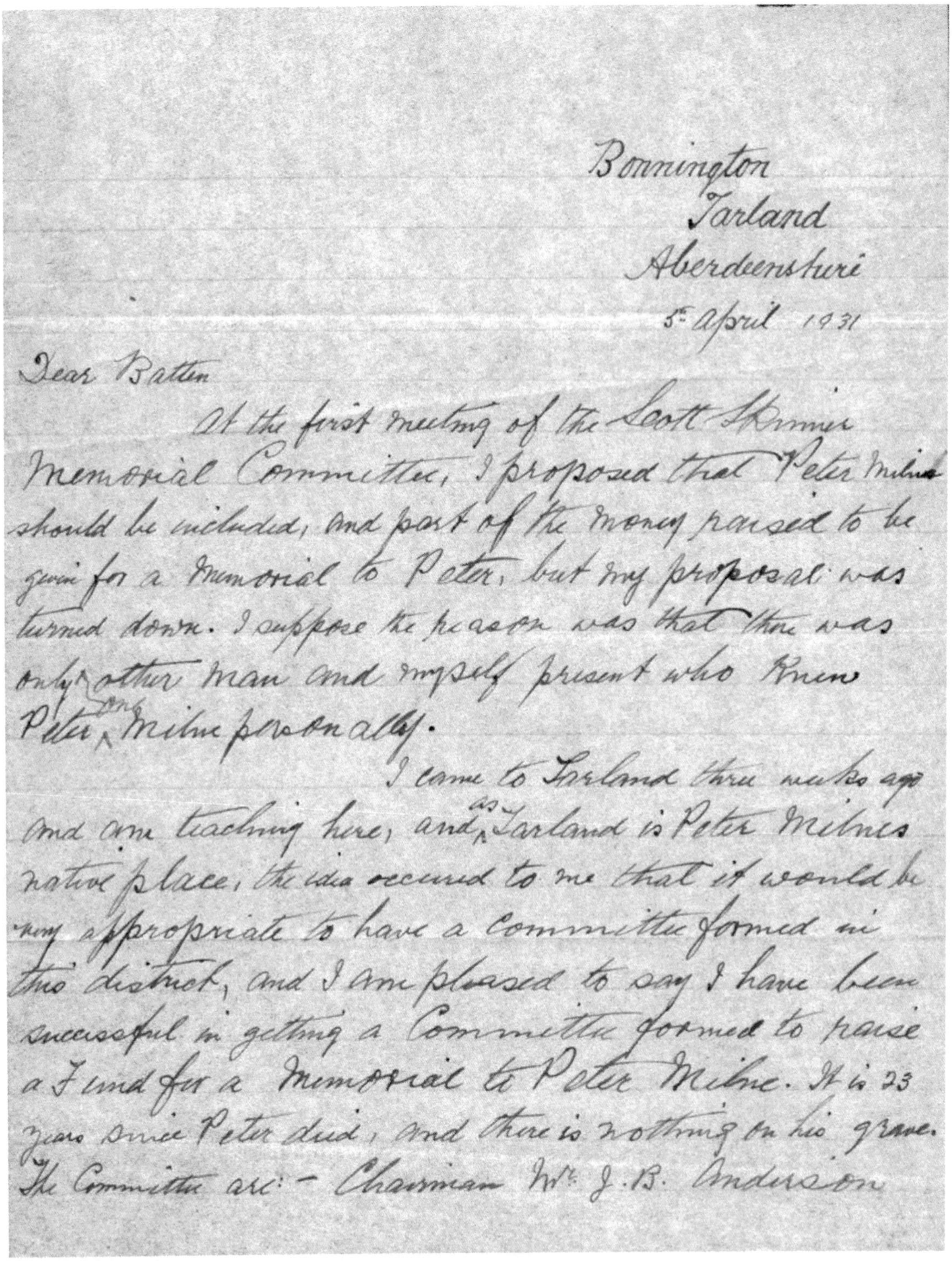

Bonnington
Tarland
Aberdeenshire
5ᵗʰ April 1931

Dear Batten

At the first meeting of the Scott Skinner
Memorial Committee, I proposed that Peter Milne
should be included, and part of the money raised to be
given for a memorial to Peter, but my proposal was
turned down. I suppose the reason was that there was
only other man and myself present who knew
Peter Milne personally.

I came to Tarland three weeks ago
and am teaching here, and as Tarland is Peter Milnes
native place, the idea occurred to me that it would be
very appropriate to have a Committee formed in
this district, and I am pleased to say I have been
successful in getting a Committee formed to raise
a Fund for a memorial to Peter Milne. It is 23
years since Peter died, and there is nothing on his grave.
The Committee are:— Chairman Mr. J. B. Anderson

Letter to Grant from George Rose Wood, 5 April 1931, page 1.

128

Schoolhouse, Logie Coldstone, and Messrs
G Rose Wood, Aberdeen; A. K. Henderson, Torphins;
John Knowles, Ballater; Wm Anderson, Tarland;
and Alex Innes, Tarland.

I am enclosing a subscription
Sheet, and we shall be very grateful of your assistance.
I am sure a good many members of your Band would
give a small subscription. Could you not get up a
Concert in aid of the Fund in some small Town in
your district, such as Inverofford, or Beauly. I am
organising a Series of Concerts in this district in aid
of the Fund. The opening Concert is fixed for the 24th April
at Tarland. The Aberdeen Strathspey & Reel Society
Band are coming to the Tarland Concert. I am also
arranging for Concerts at Logie Coldstone, Dennet,
Towie and Strathdon.

Our object in raising this Fund is to
get a modest Memorial Stone for Peter Milne's grave and
to publish all his unpublished Music. The best of
Peter's Compositions are unpublished. I have a
number of them, but since I came to Tarland Mr

Letter to Grant from George Rose Wood, 5 April 1931, page 2.

Also Innes, Boot Maker, who was a pupil of Peters and a great friend and enthusiast, has shown me a whole lot of Peter's unpublished compositions that I had never seen before, some of them very pretty; particularly "Bonnie Aboyne". I will send you a copy of this beautiful melody. I am to play it at the concerts. It would be a great pity to allow these beautiful unpublished melodies of Peters to get lost, as no doubt they would if they are not published.

I have written a short history of Peter Milnes life, which will appear in the Aberdeen Press and Journal, I expect tomorrow, so look out for it. Peter Milne was extremely modest, kind hearted, and a most lovable man. I have sent a photo of Peters to the Press which will appear if they manage to reproduce it.

I hope you are keeping well, and with kindest regards

Yours faithfully
G Rose Wood

Letter to Grant from George Rose Wood, 5 April 1931, page 3.

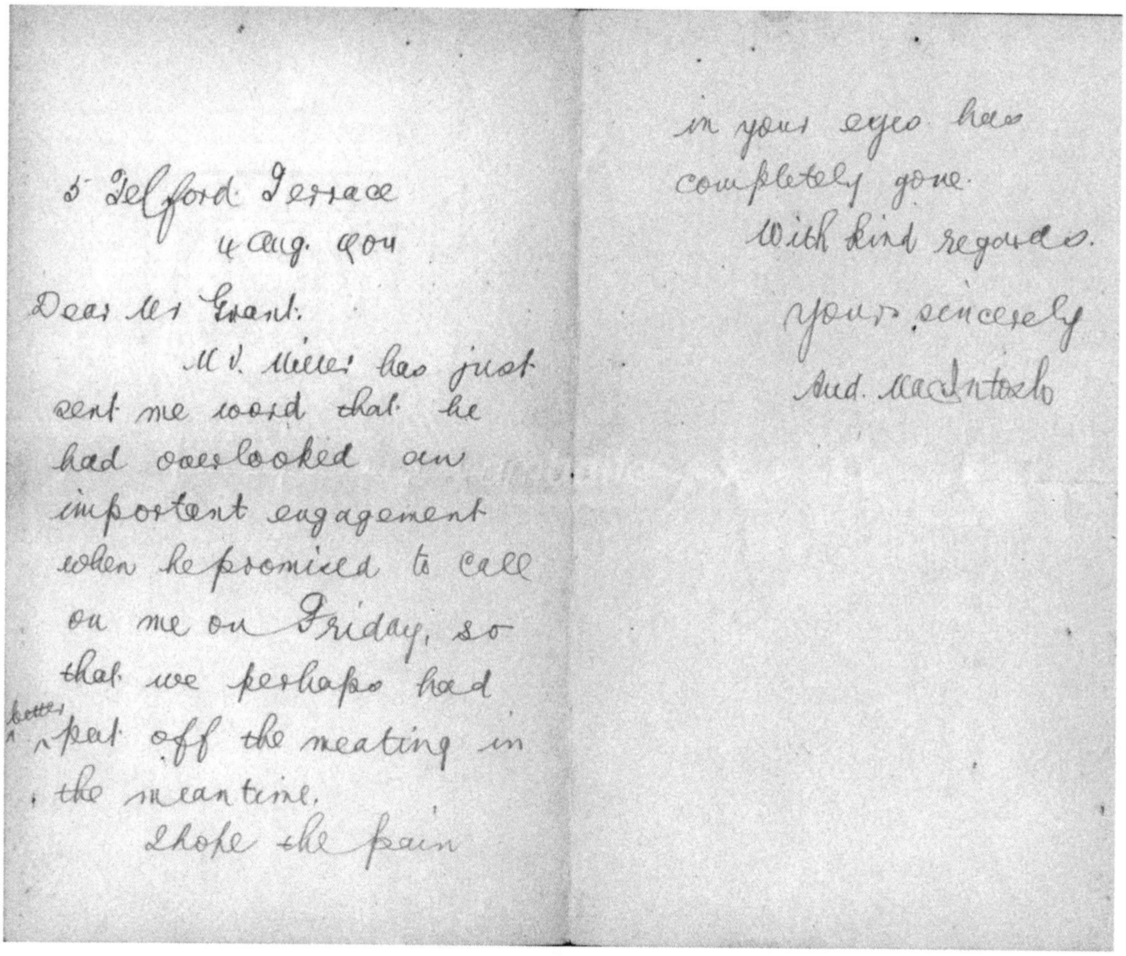

5 Telford Terrace
4 Aug. 1904

Dear Mr Grant.

Mr V. Mills has just sent me word that he had overlooked an important engagement when he promised to call on me on Friday, so that we perhaps had better put off the meeting in the meantime.

I hope the pain in your eyes has completely gone.

With kind regards.

Yours sincerely

And. MacIntosh

Letter to Grant from Andrew MacIntosh, 4 Aug 1904.

The Cottage,

Elsing, Dereham.

5th. March. 1925.

62 Oxford St.

London W.

My. Dear Baillie.

What. do. you. think
of. your. vibration. system. now.
It. is. only. the 2d story. from. Croft.
to. University.

How. are. you. getting. on. I
have. not. heard. anything. of. you. for
so. long. that. I. am. beginning. to. wonder.
what. your. old. face. is. like, Do. you.
have. as. many. victories. as. ever, I
read. in. the. Inverness. Courier.
some. time. ago. that. you. are. still. going.
strong, I. may. be. in. the. north. for. a
few. days. shortly, so. string. up. your.
old. fiddle, in. Holland. Park. form

Letter to Grant from W. M. Fraser, 5 March 1925, page 1.

This letter dated 5 March 1925 was sent to Grant by his friend William MacKenzie Fraser, one time Honorary Treasurer of the London Inverness-shire Association. Mr. MacKenzie sends his regards and asks whether there have been further developments with the 'Grant Vibration Rod'. He also enquires after 'The Strathspey King', Scott Skinner.

not forgetting old Neil MacKay and the Piper from the Caledonian School that went to sleep in the bath instead of his bed, and the old jobber who went up the hill backwards &

Alick MacKenzie is up north somewhere between Aviemore & Inverness

Did you do anything further about your vibration Bow, you ought to

I called over to see the Ritchies some time ago, both the boys are married and the poor old mother died some time ago.

Any word of the King I have not heard about him for some time

With kindest regards to all at home from your

Auld friend

William MacKenzie Fraser

Letter to Grant from W. M. Fraser, 5 March 1925, page 2.

London Inverness-shire Association.

President - The MACKINTOSH OF MACKINTOSH.

Vice-Presidents:

"AIR SON MATH NA GIORRACHD"

THE RIGHT HON. LORD LOVAT.
SIR ROBERT B. FINLAY, K.C., M.P.
SIR GEORGE MACPHERSON GRANT, BART.
SIR JOHN STIRLING-MAXWELL, BART., M.P.
DONALD CAMERON, Esq., of Lochiel,
     Lord Lieutenant of Inverness-shire.
SIR DONALD CURRIE, G.C.M.G.
JAMES E. B. BAILLIE, Esq., of Dochfour.

W. D. MACKENZIE, Esq., of Farr and Newbie.
THE BISHOP OF ARGYLL AND THE ISLES.
THE VEN. W. MACDONALD SINCLAIR, D.D.,
    Archdeacon of London.
A. LEE INNES, Esq.
THE REV. DR. DONALD MACLEOD, M.A.
MACLEOD of Macleod.
THE RT. HON. LORD TWEEDMOUTH.

THE REV. ALBERT V. BAILLIE, M.A.
CHARLES CLARK, Esq.
ANGUS MACKINTOSH, Esq., of Holme.
The Right Honourable LORD STRATHCONA and
    MOUNT ROYAL, G.C.M.G.; P.C.
W. SOPPER, Esq., of Dunmaglass.
RUARI C. GOODEN-CHISHOLM, Esq.
COLONEL JOHN S. YOUNG.

Honorary Treasurers:

DONALD C. FRASER, 24, KING STREET, HAMMERSMITH, W.
W. MACKENZIE FRASER, 9, CLARENDON ROAD, HOLLAND PARK, W.

Honorary Secretaries:

JAMES DOAK, 16, MARK LANE, E.C.
DONALD H. FRASER, 5, RANGOON STREET, E.C.

14th April 1902

Dear Mr Grant,

The London Inverness-shire Assoc
are going to hold a Concert in the Queens Hall
on the 3rd July.

I have suggested to the Committee that
you should be asked to give a selection
of Highland Music on the Violon

I have heard you play several times
and feel sure that you would take well.

Will you kindly let me know by return
if you would be willing to come and
what your expenses would be.

Have you heard that your friend

Letter to Grant from W. M. Fraser, 14 April 1902, page 1.

This letter dated 14 April 1902 was sent to Grant from William MacKenzie Fraser, at that time Honorary Treasurer of the London Inverness-shire Association. In the letter, Mr. Fraser invites Mr. Grant to perform at a forthcoming concert in the Queens Hall, London.

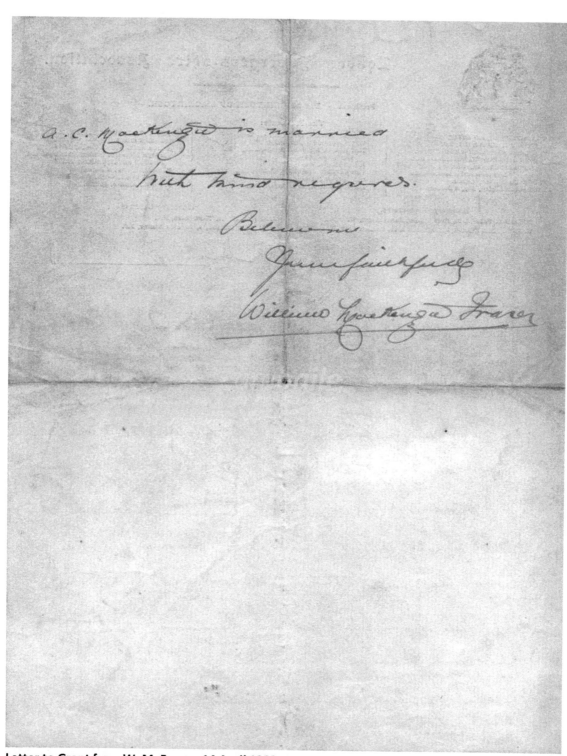

A.C. Mackenzie is married

with kind regards.

Believe me

Yours faithfully

William Mackenzie Fraser

Letter to Grant from W. M. Fraser, 14 April 1902, page 2 .

25th Sept 1935

Subscription list in aid of a
wreath etc in memory of the late
Mr David McCaskill by members
of the Highland Strathspey & Reel Society

Alexr Grant	Paid	-	5	.
J. McPherson	Paid	-	5	.
Duncan Grant	Paid		5	.
Hugh McDonald	Paid	-	5	.
E. C. Jack	Paid	-	5	.
Donald Riddell	Paid	-	4	.
B. G. Hoare	Paid	-	2	6
Ian Grant	Paid	-	3	.
Wm Fraser Muirtown	Paid	-	2	6
Rod. Mackenzie	Paid		2	6
K. Tuach	Paid	-	2	6
Peter McDonald, Loch Duich Hotel	Paid	-	2	6
Secretary	Paid	-	2	6
Wm Mackay, Clachnaharry	Paid	-	2	6
Mrs Davidson	Paid	-	2	6
George Bell	Paid	-	2	6
Duncan Cameron "County"	Paid	-	5	.
John Brown	Paid	-	2	6
Tom. Gordon	Paid	-	2	6
A. Gair	Paid	-	2	6
James Morrison	Paid	-	2	6
James Ritchie	Paid	-	2	6
James McBean	Paid	-	2	6
Wm Mackay	Paid	-	2	6
J. D. Wheatley	Paid	-	2	6
Alexr Fraser & John Fraser	Paid	-	5	.
D. Morison, Beauly	Paid	-	10	-
J. McDougall	Paid	-	2	6
Per Duncan Grant 1 Friend	Paid	.	5	.
do. do.	Paid	.	2	6
Duncan Mackenzie, Beeston	Paid	.	2	6
Arthur Mackenzie	Paid	.	2	6
Chas. Lemon	Paid	.	2	6
	£	5	12	.

Highland Strathspey & Reel Society, accounts sheet, 1935.

Strathspey and Reel Societies have been a common feature of the traditional music scene in Scotland since the formation of the first society in Edinburgh in 1881. The Highland branch was formed in 1903. One of its founder members, Alexander Grant (also known as 'Battan') was leader of the society right up until his death in 1942, a period of almost forty years. This accounts sheet dated 25 September 1935 shows a subscription list in aid of a wreath etc., in memory of the late Mr. David McCaskill. Donations from members of the Highland Strathspey and Reel Society amount to £5 12s. Included in the list are donations from Alexander Grant, Donald Riddell, and Donald Morison.

Highland Strathspey & Reel Society, Competition Programme 1905, page 3.

This typed programme is for a Highland Strathspey and Reel Concert at Croy, 6th April 1928. The programme includes solo violin performances from Alexander Grant and songs from various people including Miss MacLeod and Mr. Black. The society opens and closes the concert with 'Highland Selections'.

Highland Strathspey & Reel Society Programme, 1932, page 1.

This programme is for a Highland Strathspey and Reel Society Concert held on 21 June 1932, in the Central Hall, Academy Street, Inverness. The society's chairman at this time was ex-Baillie George Gallon.

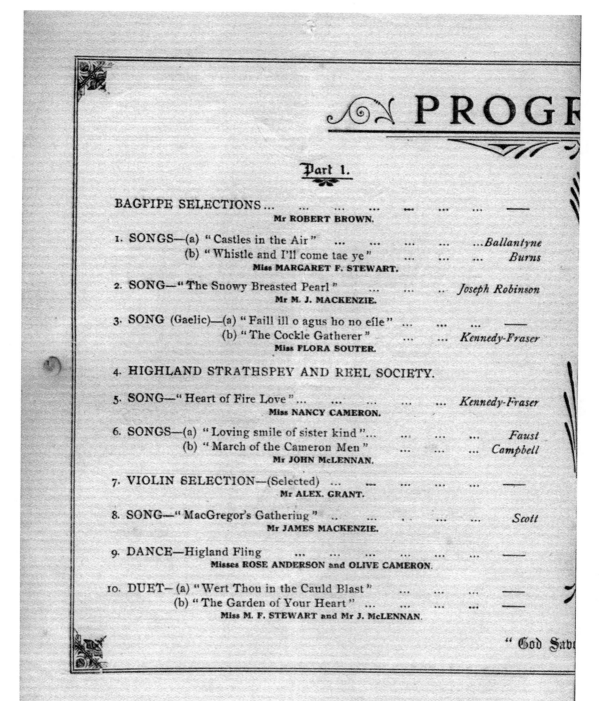

PROGR

Part 1.

BAGPIPE SELECTIONS ...   .   ---   ...   ---
Mr ROBERT BROWN.

1. SONGS—(a) "Castles in the Air" ...   .Ballantyne
   (b) "Whistle and I'll come tae ye"   ...   .   Burns
Miss MARGARET F. STEWART.

2. SONG—"The Snowy Breasted Pearl"   ...   . Joseph Robinson
Mr M. J. MACKENZIE.

3. SONG (Gaelic)—(a) "Faill ill o agus ho no eile" ...   .   ---
   (b) "The Cockle Gatherer"   ...   ... Kennedy-Fraser
Miss FLORA SOUTER.

4. HIGHLAND STRATHSPEY AND REEL SOCIETY.

5. SONG—"Heart of Fire Love" ...   . Kennedy-Fraser
Miss NANCY CAMERON.

6. SONGS—(a) "Loving smile of sister kind" ...   . Faust
   (b) "March of the Cameron Men"   ...   . Campbell
Mr JOHN McLENNAN.

7. VIOLIN SELECTION—(Selected) ...   ---   ...   .   ---
Mr ALEX. GRANT.

8. SONG—"MacGregor's Gathering" ..   .. Scott
Mr JAMES MACKENZIE.

9. DANCE—Higland Fling   ...   .   ---
Misses ROSE ANDERSON and OLIVE CAMERON.

10. DUET—(a) "Wert Thou in the Cauld Blast"   ...   .   ---
    (b) "The Garden of Your Heart" ...   .   ---
Miss M. F. STEWART and Mr J. McLENNAN.

"God Sav

Highland Strathspey & Reel Society Programme, 1932, page 2.

This programme is for a Highland Strathspey and Reel Society Concert held on 21 June 1932, in the Central Hall, Academy Street, Inverness. As well as leading the fiddlers (item 4), Mr. Grant performed a solo violin selection (item 7).

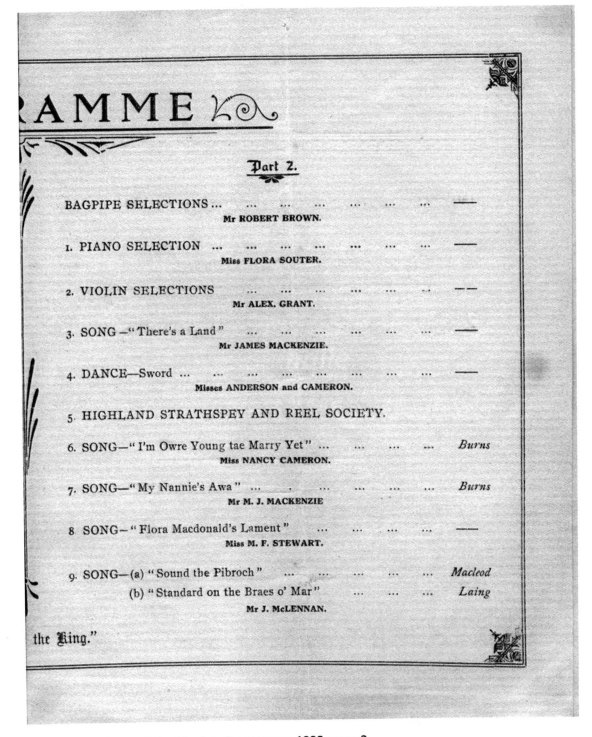

RAMME

Part 2.

BAGPIPE SELECTIONS ... ... —
Mr ROBERT BROWN.

1. PIANO SELECTION ... ... —
Miss FLORA SOUTER.

2. VIOLIN SELECTIONS ... ... — —
Mr ALEX. GRANT.

3. SONG —"There's a Land" ... ... —
Mr JAMES MACKENZIE.

4. DANCE—Sword ... ... —
Misses ANDERSON and CAMERON.

5. HIGHLAND STRATHSPEY AND REEL SOCIETY.

6. SONG—"I'm Owre Young tae Marry Yet" ... ... *Burns*
Miss NANCY CAMERON.

7. SONG—"My Nannie's Awa" ... ... *Burns*
Mr M. J. MACKENZIE

8. SONG—"Flora Macdonald's Lament" ... ... —
Miss M. F. STEWART.

9. SONG—(a) "Sound the Pibroch" ... ... *Macleod*
    (b) "Standard on the Braes o' Mar" ... ... *Laing*
Mr J. McLENNAN.

the King."

Highland Strathspey & Reel Society Programme, 1932, page 3.

This programme is for a Highland Strathspey and Reel Society Concert held on 21 June 1932, in the Central Hall, Academy Street, Inverness. As well as leading the fiddlers (item 5), Mr. Grant performed a solo violin selection (item 2).

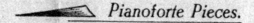
Highland Strathspey & Reel Society Programme, 1932, page 4 (advert).

This advert for 'Mrs David Logan, Pianoforte and Music Seller' appeared on the back of a programme for a Highland Strathspey and Reel Society Concert held on 21 June 1932, in the Central Hall, Academy Street, Inverness.

Highland Strathspey & Reel Society Programme, 1935, page 1.

This programme is for a Highland Strathspey and Reel Society Concert held on 12 July 1935 in the Town Hall, Inverness. Tickets are priced at one and two shillings and the accompanist is Miss Florence M. Miller.

PROGF

PART I.

1. **Bagpipe Selections** ... ... ——
   Pipe-Major John Macdonald, M.B.E.

2. **Song** (Gaelic)—" Fear a Bhata " ... ... *Traditional*
   Miss Mary Macdonald.

3. **Song**—" Border Ballad " ... ... *Cowan*
   Mr Fred Miller.

4. **March**—" Balmoral Highlanders " ... ... ——
   Strathspeys—" Highlanders Farewell " ... ... ——
    " Miss Drummond of Perth " ... ... ——
    " George the Fourth " ... ... ——
   Reels—" George the Fourth " ... ... ——
    " Cabar Feidh " ... ... ——
   Highland Strathspey and Reel Society.

5. **Song**—" Bonnie Strathyre " ... ... *Songs of the North*
   Mrs J. Thow.

6. **Dance**—Sword Dance ... ...
   Miss Olive Cameron.

7. **Songs**—(a) " Silent Worship " ... ... *Handel*
    (b) " There is a Ladye " ... ... *Winifred Bury*
   Mr M. J. Mackenzie.

8. **Song**—" The Misty Isle of Skye " ... ... *Grimshaw*
   Miss Peggy Strachan.

9. **Song**—" Maid of Morven " ... ... *Songs of the North*
   Mr Wm. Fraser.

Highland Strathspey & Reel Society Programme, 1932, page 2.

This programme is for a Highland Strathspey and Reel Society Concert held on 12 July 1935 in the Town Hall, Inverness. It includes various solo artists including Pipe Major John Macdonald M.B.E.

PART II.

1. **Bagpipe Selections** ... ... —
   Pipe-Major John Macdonald, M.B.E.

2. **Song**—" Lassie o' Mine " ... ... *Mackenzie Murdoch*
   Mrs J. Thow.

3. **Song**—" My Land " ... ... *W. S. Roddie*
   Mr Fred Miller.

4. **Song** (Gaelic)—" Far an robh mi 'n Raoir " ... ... *Neil McLeod*
   Miss Mary Macdonald.

5. **March**—" Scott Skinner's Welcome to Inverness " ... ... —
   Strathspeys—" Miss Lyall " ... ... —
      " Highland Whisky " ... ... —
      " Lady Madeline Sinclair " ... ... —
   Reels—" The Mason's Apron " ... ... —
      " Perth Hunt " ... ... —
   Highland Strathspey and Reel Society.

6. **Song**—" Land of Hope and Glory " ... ... *Elgar*
   Mr Wm. Fraser.

7. **Song**—" Just a Cottage small " ... ... —
   Miss Peggy Strachan.

8. **Dance**—Highland Fling ... ... —
   Miss Olive Cameron.

9. **Songs**—(a) " The Auld Fisher " ... ... *Hamish McCunn*
      (b) " Joy of my Heart " ... ... *Hugh S. Roberton*
   Mr M. J. Mackenzie.

GOD SAVE THE KING.

Highland Strathspey & Reel Society Programme, 1935, page 3.

This programme is for a Highland Strathspey and Reel Society Concert held on 12 July 1935 in the Town Hall, Inverness. Included in the programme are solo vocal performances by Miss Mary Macdonald and Miss Peggy Strachan.

Highland Strathspey & Reel Society Programme, 1935, page 4.

This advert for the Glen Albyn and County Hotels appeared on the back of a programme for a Highland Strathspey and Reel Society Concert held on 12 July 1935 in the Town Hall, Inverness.

ROYAL BURGH OF INVERNESS

TELEGRAPHIC ADDRESS
"TOWN CLERK"
TELEPHONE Nº 43.

JAMES CAMERON,
TOWN CLERK.

Town Clerk's Office.
Town House.
Inverness 31st August, 1936.

DMR/MF.

Mr John Fraser,
    Secretary,
        Highland Strathspey & Reel Society,
           Telford Terrace,
             INVERNESS.

Dear Sir,

<u>Ness Islands.</u>

       I have to inform you that the Entertainments Committee have arranged to hold two further Special Nights in the Ness Islands on 4th and 11th prox., and there is also a possibility that a Special Night will be held on 18th prox. in aid of the funds of the Royal Northern Infirmary. I shall therefore be glad if you can kindly arrange for the attendance of your Society to sustain the programmes on these dates.

                   Yours faithfully,

                   Town Clerk.

Letter to Secretary of Highland Strathspey & Reel Society, 1936.

In this letter dated 31 August 1936, from the Inverness Town Clerk, J. Cameron to the society's secretary, John Fraser, a request is being made for the society's attendance at three evening concerts arranged by the council's Entertainments Committee.

Highland Strathspey & Reel Society Programme, 1911, page 1.

This programme is for a Highland Strathspey and Reel Society Annual Concert held on 24 February 1911, in the Music Hall, Inverness. At this time, the society's president was Neil D. Mackintosh of Raigmore. Concert tickets are priced at two shillings, one and sixpence, and sixpence.

... PROGR

Part I.

1. SELECTION - - - - HIGHLAND STRATHSPEY AND REEL SOCIETY

   Strathspeys—"Lady Mary Ramsay," "Jessie Smith," "Cameron got his Wife Again."
   Reels—"Jenny Dang the Weaver," "The Wind that Shakes the Barley."

2. SONG - - - "My Nannie, O" - Mr DOUGLAS YOUNG

3. SONG - - - "Eileen Alannah" Miss JESSIE LIVINGSTONE

4. VIOLIN SOLO - - - Mr ALEX. GRANT, Leader of H.S. and R.S.

5. SONG - "Tell me, Mary, how to Woo Thee" Mr DONALD FRASER

6. DANCE - - - "Highland Fling" Messrs MACPHERSON & MACNEILL

7. SONG - - - - - - - Miss KATE MACDONALD

8. COMPETITION—VIOLIN

   1st Prize—Gold Pendant, presented by an anonymous donor for playing of a Strathspey and
   Reel of Scott Skinner's compositions.

   2nd Prize—Presented by Messrs Marr Wood & Co.

9. DUET - - - Miss JESSIE LIVINGSTONE and Mr DOUGLAS YOUNG

ACCOMPANIST - - - -

Highland Strathspey & Reel Society Programme, 1911, page 2.

This programme is for a Highland Strathspey and Reel Society Annual Concert held on 24 February 1911, in the Music Hall, Inverness. As well as leading the fiddlers (item 1), Mr. Grant performs a violin solo (item 4).

AMME ...

PART II.

1. SONG - - - "Macgregor's Gathering" - Mr Douglas Young

2. SELECTION - - - - Highland Strathspey and Reel Society
   Strathspeys—" Miller of Drone," "South of the Grampians" " Earl Gray."
   Reels —" Mrs Macleod of Raasay," "High Road to Linton."

3. SONG - - - "Il Bacio" (*Arditi*) - Miss Jessie Livingstone

4. COMPETITION—PIANO - Strathspeys and Reels by any Composer
   1st Prize—Gold Medal—Presented by Highland Strathspey and Reel Society.
   2nd Prize—Collection of Music, value 15s—Presented by Messrs Logan & Co., Church Street.

5. SONG - - "Doon the Burn, Davie, Lad" Miss Kate Macdonald

6. DANCE - - Highland Reel {Misses M. Fraser and W. Macneill
                              {Messrs Macpherson and Macneill

7. SONG - - - "Good-Bye" (*Tosti*) Miss Jessie Livingstone

PRESENTATION OF PRIZES.

8. SONG - - - "The Distant Shore" - - Mr Douglas Young

9. VIOLIN SOLO - - - - Mr A. Grant, Leader of H.S. and R.S.

- - - Mrs WHITEHEAD.

Highland Strathspey & Reel Society Programme, 1911, page 3.

This programme is for a Highland Strathspey and Reel Society Annual Concert held on 24 February 1911, in the Music Hall, Inverness. As well as leading the fiddlers (item 2), Mr. Grant concludes the evening with a violin solo (item 9).

Academy Street showing the Empire Theatre or Picture House

(Courtesy of Inverness Field Club – Old Inverness in Pictures)

To the Members of the
Highland Strathspey & Reel Society.

I have gone carefully over the Document embodying the donor's money gift to establish a "competition" in Strathspeys and Reels by the Highland Strathspey & Reel Society and have to make the following remarks thereanent:

The object the donor has mainly in view appears to be to aim at perfect playing, to recover old tunes and encourage the production of New. — Three entirely different departments, demanding seperate gifts and abilities. As such it is collectively outwith the scope and possibilities of a Society of players, whose business and purport is to produce musical rendering.

The Society therefore must per se decline a competition in which original Composition or literary research are made conditions. These involve special gifts and advantages in which individual members of a collective body can hardly

---

Letter to Members of Highland Strathspey & Reel Society, 1927, page 1.

This letter (page 1) to the Highland branch from Mr. B.G. Hoare, dated 21 October 1927, refers to a sum of money donated to the society for the establishment of a competition in 'Strathspeys and Reels'. It is Mr. Hoare's opinion that the society decline the offer; the donor adds too many restrictive conditions. Mr. Hoare concludes by conjecturing whether the donor is, in fact, a local celebrity.

be expected to be (endowed). Originality[2]
in any form belongs only to genius
and is extremely rare.

With regard to the playing rules,
I would again remark that you cannot
go outside the rules that apply to an
Art itself. Tradition and practice has
already fixed the form of both Strathspey
and Reel. You may take a different
type of setting, say Neil Gow's, Kerr's
or Scott-Skinner's (the latter the best
undoubtedly for reasons, which I cant
enter into at present) but you cannot "vary"
it without destroying its content as a
dance tune. Variations are reserved for
Marches, (Pibrochs) Laments (Coronachs)
+c. Here you have a slow air which
can be "varied" in notation and "time"
without destroying its form. The Strathspey
and Reel demand absolute conformity
to its pattern throughout. fixed by the laws
of its own content and purpose.

Changes of key as tests of musicianship

Letter to Members of Highland Strathspey & Reel Society, 1927, page 2.

are quite practicable. Only, it
should be born in mind that the reason
that two sharps (D major) and three sharps
(A major) are most commonly used is the
facility that both these keys afford of
the "open string" ~~of both~~ to ~~afford~~ the player
where rapid bowing and full toned notes
are desirable.

It would be an easy matter to make
a number of sets a full test of playing
ability, but here again there must be a
minimum — selection of new or old or
difficult sets is another matter — as time
and numbers are factors even in competition.

I think the donor's own remark;
" Our endeavour is that the collection and
the competition, will be so difficult that the
medal will seldom or ever be won " is a
correct summing up of the whole matter
viz Impossibility.

Should this however happen the testator
has a way out of the difficulty;
" No member can have more than one Gold medal,
" and in the event of the Gold Medallist winning

Letter to Members of Highland Strathspey & Reel Society, 1927, page 3.

" again, he gets a gold Bar each time he
" wins and to be attached to the gold medal".
How this can be done with £10, is an enigma
to me. The interest on £10 after buying the
first medal would be ———— a few pence.

Viewing the whole scheme, I
think it is the duty of the Highland
Strathspey & Reel Society to decline
its acceptance, as it cannot carry
out its provisions. Unless the donor
comes forward and agrees to let the
Society draw up its own ideas in
rules to govern such a competition.

The name Jomson (or Johnson ?)
and the anonymity attached to the "document"
makes one wonder if the Society is being
" ragged" under the pseudonym of a
local celebrity.

Bheh Hoare

Inverness 21 Oct 1927.

Letter to Members of Highland Strathspey & Reel Society, 1927, page 4.

Copy of letter.

"Netherdale,
Beauly
22nd Mar. /28.

Dear Morison,

Many thanks for the copy of the Ayrshire Post with report of meeting of the Ayr Sketch Club.

I am very much astonished at the way Mr. Nash is reported to have represented his connection with Mr. Grant's Rondello, for we who have been watching the development of the instrument during the past number of years know quite well that it was not merely the idea which originated with Mr. Grant, but that every detail of material, size and structure was worked out with the utmost exactness by him.

We understood that all these had been

Letter on Alexander Grant's 'Rondello', 22 March 1928, page 1.

This copy letter dated 22 March 1928, from Thomas Macdonald to D. Morison, Assistant Leader of the Highland Strathspey and Reel Society, refers to the 'Rondello', a disc-shaped violin invented by Alexander Grant, Inverness. It appears that in a recent copy of the 'Ayrshire Post', a fiddle-maker by the name of Nash has been laying claim to the invention of the 'Rondello'. Mr. Macdonald suggests the article be brought to the attention of the Highland Strathspey and Reel Society.

been sent to Nash and that he merely made a copy to measurements and instructions, as any mechanic might do.

Now, anyone who did not know the circumstances, reading the report in the Ayr paper would come to the conclusion that Nash was the man who invented the instrument (it says "made and named by him") on a hint from Grant, which you and I knew to be sheer bunkum.

Why do you not bring the report before the Strathspey & Reel Society the members of which, of course, know about Mr. Grant's invention? Surely they will rise to the occasion and do something to make it clear to the world that any credit is due to their veteran leader and to the town of Inverness and not of Ayr.

Yours etc.

(Signed) Thos. Macdonald."

Letter on Alexander Grant's 'Rondello', 22 March 1928, page 2.

This copy letter dated 22 March 1928, from Thomas Macdonald to D. Morison, Assistant Leader of the Highland Strathspey and Reel Society, refers to the 'Rondello', a disc-shaped violin invented by Alexander Grant, Inverness. It appears that in a recent copy of the 'Ayrshire Post', a fiddle-maker by the name of Nash has been laying claim to the invention of the 'Rondello'. Mr. Macdonald suggests the article be brought to the attention of the Highland Strathspey and Reel Society.

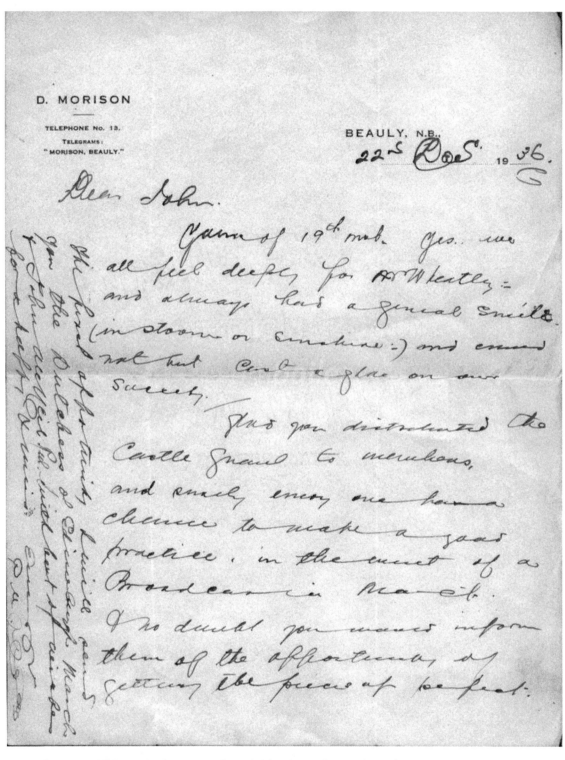

Letter from D. Morison, Assistant Leader, Highland Strathspey & Reel Society.

This letter dated 22 December 1936 is from the Highland branch Assistant Leader, Mr. D. Morison of Beauly, to 'John' (probably John Fraser, Secretary). Mr. Morison mentions three pieces of music; 'Castle Grant', 'The Duchess of Edinburgh' (march), and the 'John McNeill Reel'.

Crosbie Ho
Monkton
Prestwick   14/3/'37

To the Sec
    Inverness H.S.&R.S.

        Many thanks for the copies of Y. W. Henderson's
7/S & Melodies, I have had a job getting them.
Bayley & Ferguson to me they were out of print,
so I thought of Mr Grant and as the Yankees
say, "everything is all right". I enclose P.G.
for Books & Postage. Thanking you very
much again for the trouble you have taken
to send them to me. The Ayr S.&R. Soc
hold their 2nd Annual Concert in the
town Hall on Wednesday 17th. I trust
you have had a good season, I have only
been out playing once this season, that was
at the Kilmarnock S.&R. Soc on the 24th Feb.
My Boss is a Semi Cripple now and requires two
to help him every time he moves, Kind regards
to Mr Grant and fraternal Greetings to Inverness H.S.&R. Soc. not forgetting yourself.

                        I am
                    Your's Sincerely
                    Jas. F. McEwen.

Letter to Secretary, Highland Strathspey & Reel Society, 14 March 1937.

This letter dated 14 March 1937 is from James P. McEwen of Prestwick to the Secretary of the Highland Strathspey & Reel Society in Inverness. Mr. McEwen, a member of the Ayr Strathspey and Reel Society, was recently sent a copy of 'Flowers of Scottish Melody' (1935) from the Highland branch. He encloses £6 to cover the cost of the book and postage, and sends his kind regards to the Highland branch and its Leader, Alexander Grant.

12 Polmuir Road,
Aberdeen
12/11/36.

Dear Mrs Fraser,

Many thanks for your 30/- in P.O.'s. I'm to send order for 36 copies of the Skinner group to be posted straight to you.

Your later communication is funny. Mrs Monson is not the first Scots fiddler to read some of my _alternative_ notes as chord notes. No chords are intended at all. Since your copy is slightly different from the one I sent you last, here is the most up-to-date, pet, with Mac's strathspey in close attendance. Please send them on to D. Monson. Mind you, I think these two tunes should also be played together. It would save you & Mac. shaking hands so often (?). Pattair's one would look fine after a pipe march. I'm really proud of all three tunes, so it's up to you all to add to my pride!

Reiterated thanks. In haste
Yours sincerely.
Jn Henderson

Letter to Secretary, Highland Strathspey & Reel Society, 12 Nov 1936.

This letter dated 12 November 1936 is from Jim Murdoch Henderson, Aberdeen, to the Highland branch Secretary, Mr. John Fraser. Mr. Henderson, himself a celebrated fiddler, composer and arranger, is acknowledging receipt of Mr. Fraser's order for sheet music - 36 copies of the recently published Scott Skinner group of tunes.

12 Polmuir Road.

9 . 11 . 36 .

Dear Mr Fraser,

I had a letter from Pattan some days ago saying that your society would take 3 doz. copies of my new Scott Skinner group at 10d. each — 30/- altogether. Please send me "official" tidings so that I can order the pieces right away. Bayley & Ferguson will think that I'm trying to do them in.

I've had the enclosed airs ready for over a week. I'm confident I've given Pattan, Mac. & you three everlasting airs. You *must* get them all up for *me* also. You will have the honour to give Pattan his one: he gave you yours. By the by, the set of your air found here — perhaps slightly different from what you already have — is the one that is to go down to posterity. In fact I shall probably sometimes change its key to Bb to suit some

Letter, Highland Strathspey & Reel Society, 9 Nov 1936, page 1.

162

This letter (page 1) dated 9 November 1936 is from Jim Murdoch Henderson, Aberdeen, to the Highland branch Secretary, Mr. John Fraser. Mr. Henderson, himself a celebrated fiddler, composer and arranger, is requesting an official order for sheet music recently (unofficially) requested by 'Battan'. He also encloses three recently composed 'everlasting airs' specifically for Mr. MacPherson, Mr. Fraser, and 'Battan' Grant.

groups. J. Hardie will broadcast it next year, I hope. Pattan's tune is credited to be the best pipe strathspey composed since "Maggie Cameron". MacPherson's strathspey should sound very well indeed with the band. I have the habit of composing airs that are suitable more for good soloists rather than bands. The same cannot be said of any of the three airs now presented to the Big Three. Mac's air is a gem too.

I hope this note reaches you before your practice tomorrow so that you can break the news gently and compel all the players to take off their hats to you. Posterity will not have far to seek for a reason for my intimate association with your organisation. I always favour those who play for the sake of helping the cause rather than with the prime object of lining their own pockets. If I'm anything at all in music I'm patriotic and take much pleasure in considering your lot of enthusiasts the same.

Kindest regards to all.

Yours ever faithfully,

J. Murdoch Henderson

Letter, Highland Strathspey & Reel Society, 9 Nov 1936, page 2.

THE GLASGOW EVENING NEWS.

8 Dec. 1936.

Miss Alexander gave interpretations of these
songs which made the recital one of the most
interesting and enjoyable we have heard for
a long time.

The singerstone was always beautiful and her
outlook musical in every detail, in a long and
varied list of songs.   She gave us splendid
phrasing and real insight into the many moods
of the songs.

THE GLASGOW HERALD.

8 Dec. 1936.

Miss Alexander had previously won her place
in Glasgow as a pianist and it was equally
unlooked for and delightful to find her
displaying all the virtues of a fine singer
of Lieder.

In the thirty songs a considerable range of
mood was covered and always the result was
eloquent and made impressive by its sincerity.

This letter (page 1) dated 15 December 1936 is from Joan Alexander, L.R.A.M., A.R.C.M., to the Highland branch Secretary, Mr. John Fraser. Miss Alexander is an experienced soprano singer. She asks to be considered for an engagement with the society and encloses critiques from a recent recital in Glasgow.

CRAIGMONIE,

INVERNESS, 10th December, 1913.

Dear Sir,

I am obliged for your letter of yesterday, informing me that the Highland Reel and Strathspey Society are to hold their annual concert on Thursday evening, 25th December (Christmas Day) in the Music Hall, and asking me to act as Chairman on the occasion. I am very sorry that I am unable to do so. For many years Mrs. Mackay and myself have had a gathering of relatives and friends on Christmas Day, and the invitations for the coming Christmas dinner have already been sent out.

I am,

Yours faithfully,

William Mackay

Mr. J. Fraser,
   3 Telford Terrace,
      INVERNESS.

Letter to Secretary, Highland Strathspey & Reel Society, 1936, page 1.

This letter to the society, dated 10 December 1913, is from Mr. William MacKay, Craigmonie, Inverness. Mr. Mackay has been asked to chair the forthcoming society annual concert in the Music Hall on 25 December. Unfortunately he is unable to attend as he has a prior engagement.

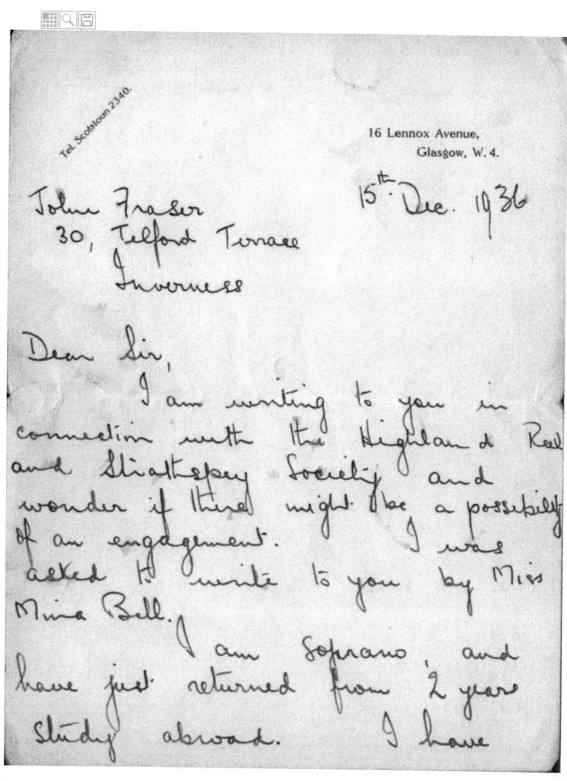

Tel. Scotstoun 2340.

16 Lennox Avenue,
Glasgow, W. 4.

John Fraser
30, Telford Terrace
Inverness

15th. Dec. 1936

Dear Sir,

I am writing to you in connection with the Highland Reel and Strathspey Society and wonder if there might be a possibility of an engagement. I was asked to write to you by Miss Mina Bell.

I am Soprano, and have just returned from 2 years study abroad. I have

Letter to Secretary, Highland Strathspey & Reel Society, 1936, page 1.

This letter (page 1) dated 15 December 1936 is from Joan Alexander, L.R.A.M., A.R.C.M., to the Highland branch Secretary, Mr. John Fraser. Miss Alexander is an experienced soprano singer. She

167

asks to be considered for an engagement with the society and encloses critiques from a recent recital in Glasgow.

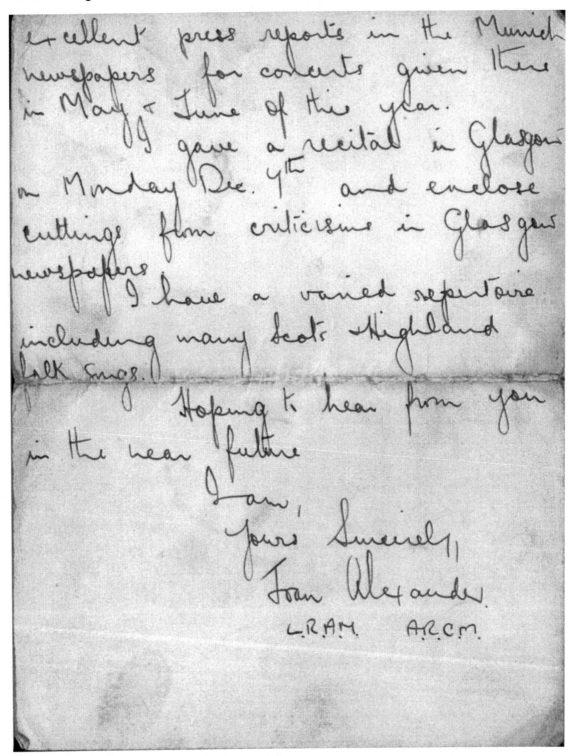

excellent press reports in the Munich newspapers for concerts given there in May & June of this year.

I gave a recital in Glasgow on Monday Dec. 4th and enclose cuttings from criticisms in Glasgow newspapers.

I have a varied repertoire including many Scots & Highland folk songs.

Hoping to hear from you in the near future

I am,

Yours Sincerely,

Joan Alexander.

L.R.A.M.   A.R.C.M.

Letter to Secretary, Highland Strathspey & Reel Society, 1936, page 2.

P.S. You'll have your Skinner group
from P.T. & J. by now.

𝕳

~~37 Westburn Road,~~ 12 Polmuir Road,
Aberdeen.

16·11·86.

Dear Mrs Fraser,

Man, ye're a thorough chiel.
I admire you all the more for that.

You will see from your copy herewith
returned that "John Fraser" is a very flexible
reel. Although the set I gave you to present to
D. Morison is probably the set that will appear
in my next collection, 1960, the other set
is not unpleasant and may be preferred by some.
I have used pencil this time to distinguish one
grouping of notes from the other. The "D" you saw
in the original copy must have been an echo
of the later picture to be introduced in 5b.
If you can't follow me now, you'll have to
come along for a week's tuition!

I haven't heard yet how Patton and
MacPherson are taking to their latest treasures.
Tell them not to be so shy.

Regards in haste,
Pd. Murdoch Henderson

Letter to Secretary, Highland Strathspey & Reel Society, 16 Nov 1936.

This letter dated 16 November 1936 is from Jim Murdoch Henderson, Aberdeen, to the Highland branch Secretary, Mr. John Fraser. Mr. Henderson, himself a celebrated fiddler, composer and arranger, has recently sent three of his latest compositions; 'everlasting airs' specifically written for Mr. MacPherson, Mr. Fraser, and 'Battan' Grant. He asks how these compositions are being received.

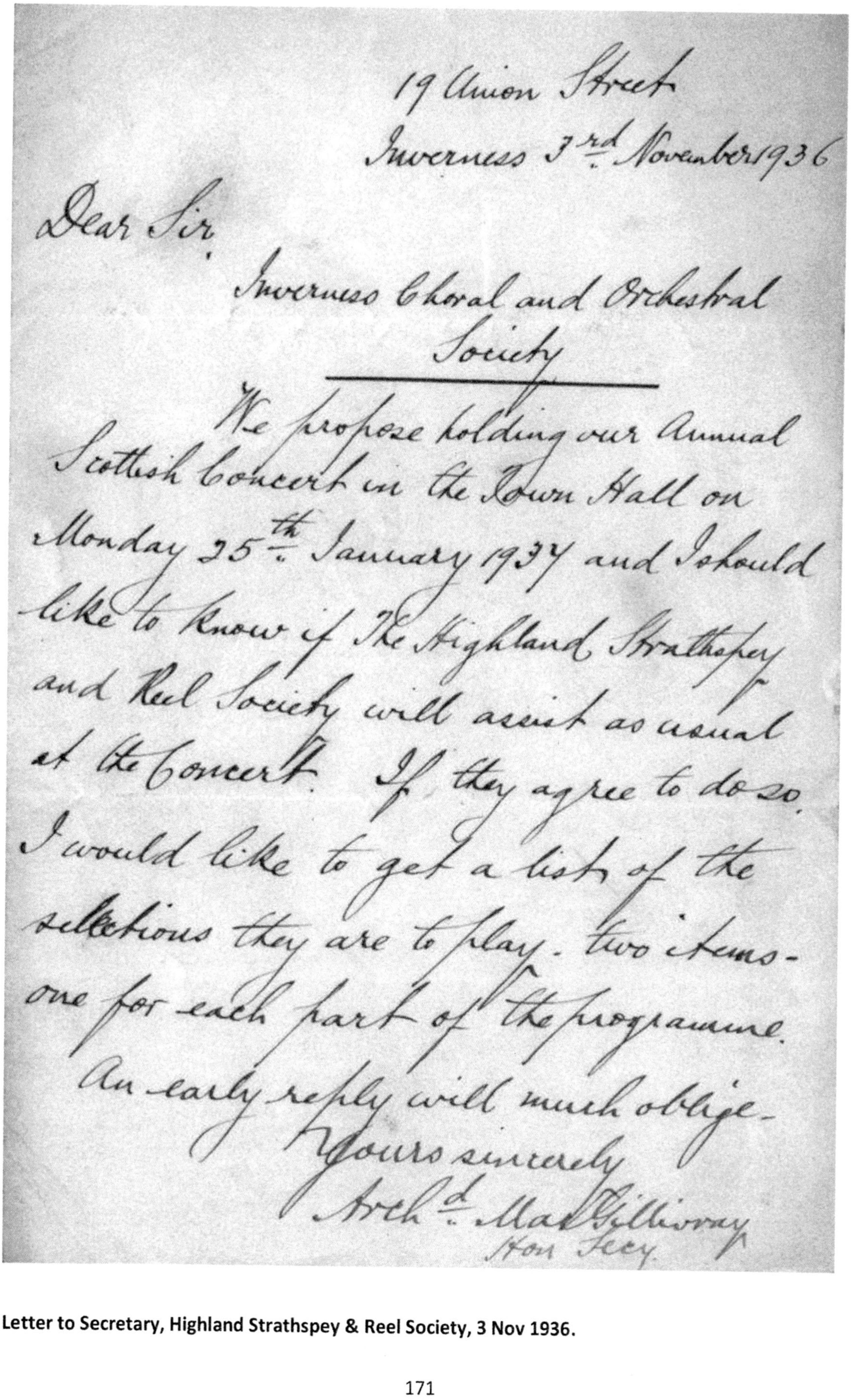

19 Union Street
Inverness 3rd November 1936

Dear Sir,

Inverness Choral and Orchestral
Society

We propose holding our Annual
Scottish Concert in the Town Hall on
Monday 25th January 1937 and I should
like to know if The Highland Strathspey
and Reel Society will assist as usual
at the Concert. If they agree to do so,
I would like to get a list of the
selections they are to play. Two items –
one for each part of the programme.

An early reply will much oblige –

Yours sincerely

Archd. MacGillivray
Hon Secy.

Letter to Secretary, Highland Strathspey & Reel Society, 3 Nov 1936.

This letter dated 3 November 1936 is from Archibald MacGillivray, Honorary Secretary of the Inverness Choral and Orchestral Society, to the Highland branch Secretary, Mr. John Fraser. Mr. MacGillivray requests that the Highland Strathspey and Reel Society assist at the forthcoming Annual Scottish Concert of the Choral Society.

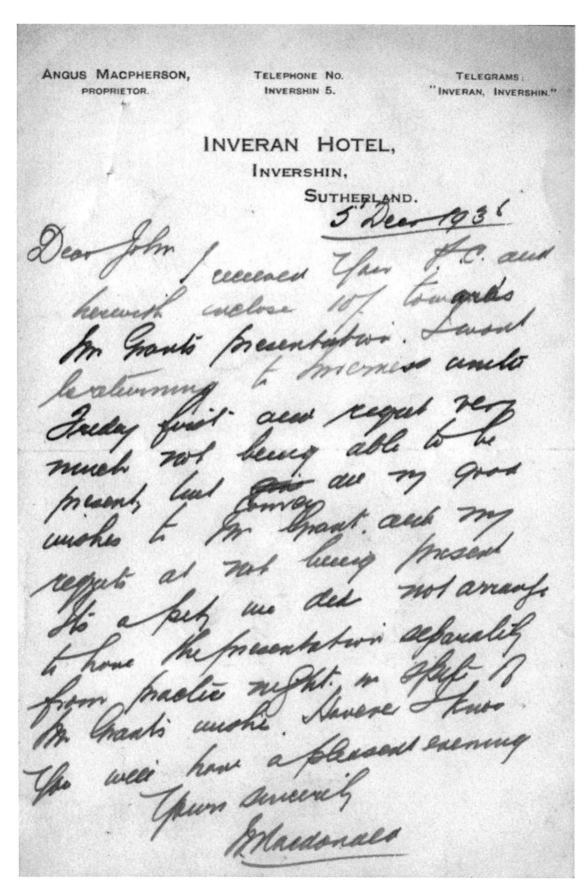

INVERAN HOTEL,
INVERSHIN,
SUTHERLAND.

5 Decr 1936

Dear John

I received Your P.C. and herewith enclose 10/ towards Mr Grant's presentation. I was returning to Inverness until Friday first, and regret very much not being able to be present, but am all my good wishes to convey to Mr Grant. and my regret at not being present

It's a pity we did not arrange to have the presentation apart from practice night, in spite of Mr Grant's wishes. However I know you will have a pleasant evening

Yours sincerely

Macdonald

Letter to Secretary, Highland Strathspey & Reel Society, 5 Nov 1936.

This letter dated 5 November 1936 is from Mr. J. MacDonald (probably Pipe-Major John MacDonald) to the Highland branch Secretary, Mr. John Fraser. In it, Mr. MacDonald expresses his regret at being unable to attend a forthcoming presentation to Mr. Grant. He encloses ten shillings to put towards the event.

42 ROSS AVENUE,
INVERNESS.

10 - 11 · 36 ·

J. Fraser Esq,
Secretary,
Highland Strathspey & Reel Society.

Dear Mr Fraser.

I hasten to write
to thank you most heartily for
the gift of Cigarettes which I
received to day.

Please convey to your Society my
most sincere thanks for such an
acceptable present, and for the
kind thoughts which prompted it.
Wishing you all success in
the future. Yours Sincerely,
J. Mackenzie.

Letter to Secretary, Highland Strathspey & Reel Society, 10 Nov 1936.

This letter dated 10 November 1936 is from Mr. J. MacKenzie, 42 Ross Avenue, Inverness, to the Highland branch Secretary, Mr. John Fraser. In it, Mr. MacKenzie expresses his gratitude for the gift of cigarettes he has recently received from the society.

Donald R. Riddell

1909 - 1992

(A Donald Riddell violin on display at IMAG)

Part 3

His Fiddle and Piping Life

Donald R. Riddell – Piper, Violin Maker and Teacher

Donald Riddell – His Background

Donald Riddell was born in 1909 in Wales, where his father was a gamekeeper, but moved with his mother to Scotland after his father was killed at the Battle of the Somme in July 1916. They settled first in the Black Isle and then moved due west to the Aird of Inverness. Donald went to school at Inverness Royal Academy and, afterwards 'served his time' as a cabinet-maker.

Donald's musical talents were many: piper, fiddle player, fiddle teacher, composer and violin maker. He was taught to play the violin by Professor Tom Davies of Inverness but taught to play the fiddle by Alexander 'Battan' Grant, an authority on the bowing of Highland music – especially strathspeys. 'Battan' also introduced young Donald to violin making.

There exists on the AmBaile web site (www.ambaile.org.uk) an audio recording of Donald re-counting his early years. In this audio extract, Donald discusses his early childhood experiences of the fiddle. He also talks about those who influenced him, notably Alexander Battan Grant, his great friend whom he held in the highest esteem.

"I always wanted to play a fiddle long before I went to school and I'd heard about the great Stradivari and other famous people, and also about Scott Skinner and people like that, and I was terribly keen to learn to play the fiddle. And there was a fiddle in the house but I wasn't allowed to touch it, so, I got a piece of wood and made a very crude little fiddle out of it which actually played. It sounded like the kettle singing at the fireside, actually, but after that I started to play by ear and when my mother heard that, she just went straight off and handed me the fiddle.

But having started off as a fiddle maker then, before I went to school, of a kind, I never forgot that and the desire to make fiddles was always with me. And it wasn't 'till quite a long time after that when I was a teenager that I really took up the idea again and of course by this time I had met Alexander Grant Battan of the vibration rod fame and he must have seen something in me because he took an interest in me - more than he took in most people - and he showed me an awful lot about it and I wouldn't make fiddles so well today if it wasn't for him, the most remarkable man I ever met".

It is surprising that Donald never met Scott Skinner but would have learned a lot about him from Sandy Battan. Donald would have been eighteen years old at the time of Skinner's death, and given that Skinner was a frequent visitor to Donald Morison's shop in Beauly, played relatively frequently at Society Concerts in Inverness, and even in the Phipps Hall in Beauly, one would have thought that there would have been plenty of opportunities to do so.

However, according to recorded voice interviews given later in his life this did not come about – i.e. an opportunity for two great giants of the Highland traditional fiddling community to meet, greet and exchange views, and friendship never came about. In his own words the nearest to this happening was one evening he observed a constant stream of cars travelling along the road past Kirkhill to Inverness – "usually you would only see about one car an hour passing. I asked someone what was on and was told that the great Scott Skinner was playing at a concert in Inverness".

By today's terms, the Moor of Clunes and Donald's Croft seem no great distance from Beauly and Inverness. However, Donald's mode of transport was likely to have been – by foot, bicycle, or horse drawn cart, there was no public transport to speak of, and he would likely not have had access to a horse, car, or convenient lift.

[**Life in Those Times**:

Though neither Lord Lovat (14th) nor his wife could drive, he owned one of the first motor cars in the district, a decapotable Chrysler registered ST3. Usually the first to adopt new advances he was pipped at the post by MacIntosh of MacIntosh who had ST1, and Cameron of Locheil who had ST2. A photograph of his later car, a 10-horsepower French-built Panhard et Levassor, being driven in Inverness in December 1903 is shown in Inverness Remembered, Vol. IV, printed by the Inverness Courier.

Lord Lovat's car – ST9 in Inverness, 1903. Note, the road does not have a tar macadam surface.

One hundred and seventeen years later the registration ST9, and still in the ownership of the Lovat Fraser family, can still be seen on a car being driven around Beauly today. (ST6, 7, and 8 were registered to an Inverness Doctor's practice)].

A Highland Fiddler and Pupil of Alexander Battan Grant
Prior to the war, Donald assisted Sandy Battan in running the Inverness Highland Strathspey and Reel Society until the war years intervened. Later, around 1973, Donald resurrected the Society (Alexander Grant having passed away in 1942), and he built up a considerable local

reputation for himself based upon his leadership and natural teaching skills. One can well imagine that with his military background of being a Pipe Major in the Lovat Scouts, he would have possessed the necessary authoritarian set of skills to achieve what he did with the band. However, synchronised bowing apart, there is no evidence to suggest that he applied the same methods when teaching his violin pupils, and Indeed, by all accounts quite the reverse seems to have been the case, as he was, and still is, greatly admired by all of his former pupils – particularly his method of getting his pupils to practice without the use of harsh words.

Players of all ages were welcomed to the Society

At rehearsals, members of the band were allowed to use music. However, for concert performances, only those who could play for about three hours without music were allowed onto the stage. This was a rule, (level of performance), which Donald never deviated from. At concerts, Donald held strictly to the belief that the music should be listened to – and not accompanied by the audience keeping time by stamping their feet on the floor. He was known to stop the band, turn to the audience, and make them aware that it was not permitted – after all, can you imagine an audience doing this during the performance of a classical masterpiece. A divergence one might say in the way we appreciate true greatness.

Donald Riddell at home in his latter years at Clunes Croft – early 1990's.

Donald's Croft at South Clunes, Kirkhill, near Beauly – his workshop is visible on the left.

Donald's workshop was situated above a lower storage area and pig stye.

A crofting way of life at Clunes generally involved keeping a range of farm animals, field work, and sometimes assisting a neighbour. Donald's son Geordie, (not him in the picture), though a talented musician and composer himself, focused his attention on rearing pigs.

Donald in his comfort zone in his workshop.

Donald once described his workshop 'as the most untidy one in Britain'
- a very modest man.

Anecdote – *Donald Fraser, (see Acknowledgements), once visited Donald when he was in the process of thinning a plate. He laid his thinning tool on top of the plate and they both went out. About one month later Donald visited his friend once again – and there, lying in exactly the same position was the tool as he had left it! – presumably age was starting to catch up with Donald then!*

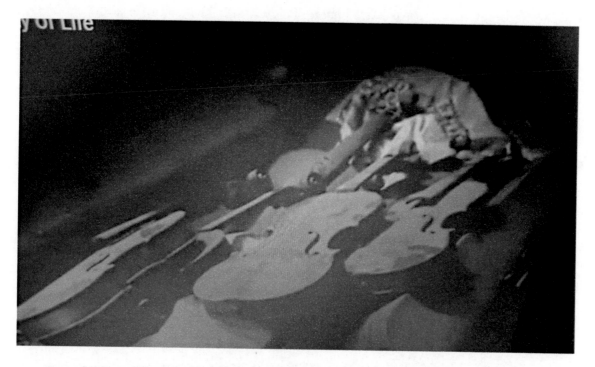

Out of this untidy dusty jumble arose some beautiful looking fiddles – see below.

Donald in his croft, and in the mirror reflection a framed print of Niel Gow can be seen. It is interesting to compare this image with the previous one of Grant at home, where one can see a large framed print of James Scott Skinner above his fireplace. These two gentlemen clearly had deep rooted interests and respect for the achievements of the key exponents of the tradition, namely Gow and Skinner. It Is however worthy of note that Skinner died two hundred years after the birth of Niel Gow, and we have had no traceable record handed down to us of how the continuity of the tradition was passed on. This on the other hand serves to highlight the importance of the Grant, Skinner, Riddell, Chisholm and MacGregor continuous heritage link which must be viewed as truly unique in Scottish Traditional fiddle music.

Historic note:

Niel Gow (1727 – 1807)

Gow came from Perthshire, having lived in the cottage where he had been born, and was renowned as a brilliant, self-taught fiddler and composer. He influenced the development of Scottish folk music. His reels and strathspeys were enjoyed across Scottish society in the late 18th century, and he was known for accompanying his playing with a sudden shout, which would startle and excite the dancers. Gow's patrons included the Duke of Atholl and Duchess of Gordon. Sir Henry Raeburn distilled many of his remarkable skills as a painter in this deeply sympathetic portrait, which is a study of intense concentration, in which all the details of texture and form are fluidly and convincingly established.

There is an audio extract on the Am Baile web-site, in which Donald talks about obtaining a good fiddle tone, a skill he learnt from Alexander Battan Grant.

"To get good tone on a fiddle, it all depends on good material in the first place, with resonant properties and knowing how to make them vibrate. A fiddle is just a wooden box of peculiar construction built as a resonator - that's all it is. And I discovered through Grant that the tone of a fiddle depends on the relationship of the front and back - a speed of taper and that relationship is determined by the thickness of the wood. But this thickness - no one can ever discover it if they've got to use callipers and mathematical instruments. You've got to measure the vibrations and you do that with your ear, just by tapping, gently tapping, or brushing the plates with your fingers you can assess the speed that they're vibrating at and get the relationship adjusted that way. Generally the thicker the wood, the higher the speed of vibration, you see, and therefore the higher the pitch and the thinner you work it, the lower it goes and there comes a time when you must know the pitch you're aiming at".

Donald taps the rear plate with the tips of his fingers whilst listening intently to the vibration of the wood.

Post War, and with his proven background, Donald went on to build on his spirited renaissance of Scots fiddle music in the Inner Moray Firth area. Having reconstituted the Inverness Strathspey and Reel Society in the 1970's, it was the members of the Society who in turn benefited from Grant's teaching of Donald Riddell that had set him off on his career as a violin maker. Donald, however, had made his first violin before he started school, and eventually about two thirds of the members of the society at one time played on his fiddles.

Pre War – Donald Riddell, when Sandy Battan led the Inverness Strathspey & Reel Society, (established by Grant in 1903), and Donald was his assistant having taken over from Donald Morison.

One of his great achievements was undoubtedly that his pupils benefitted greatly, not only from his efforts in teaching them and running the Society, but also from his craftmanship in providing many of them with violins which he made himself.

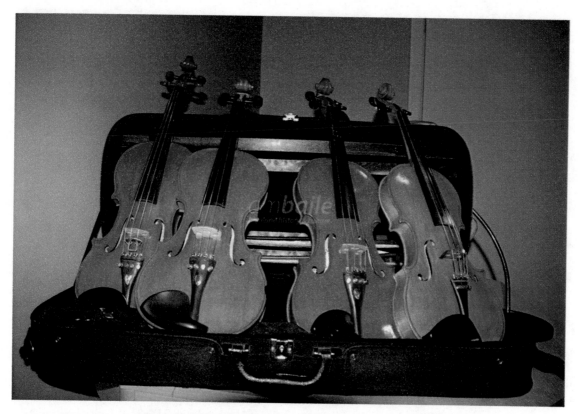

A set of violins made by Donald Riddell - three of which have a distinctive heart-shaped silver inlay below the fine tuners on the tailpiece.

The Rondello on display ay Inverness castle.

This photograph was taken at a fiddle workshop held on 15 June 2010 by Highland Council's Inverness Traditional Music Project, in partnership with Inverness Museum and Art Gallery, (Courtesy of IMAG), in which the work of Grant and Riddell were celebrated. The photograph shows, from left to right, Irene Fraser, Sara-Jane Summers, and Catharine Niven, formerly museum curator – she is holding the Rondello.

Callipers and clamps all used in the process of making a fiddle in Donald's workshop

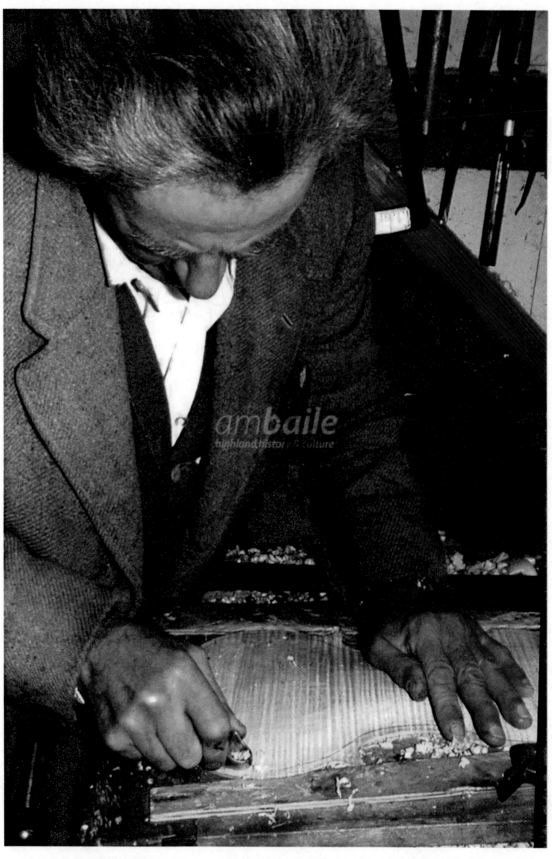

Thinning the plates – a very precise job requiring great expertise. (Take too much wood off and you cannot put it back on again!)

Donald Riddell in the process of making a fiddle. The top plate is being worked on whils't it is lying in the mould, defining the peripheral, (plan) shape of the instrument.

Donald trained as a carpenter and will have made the bench where he is working. Anyone with a keen eye for such things will note that given its apparent weight it is unlikely to wobble.

Thinning and Shaping the Plates

Achieved by removing the plate from the mould and tapping the plate with his fingers, as the process proceeds in order to give the desired frequency (vibrational) response.

It is interesting to note that among the contents of Grant's workshop held in IMAG, there is a tuning fork pitched to the key of C? – violins of course have strings tuned to G, D, A and E pitch. In a later interview Donald reveals that although there are various ways in which to fine tune the plates, he suggests that the Cremonese master fiddle makers would have used the simple method of blowing a chromatic scale into the f-hole. The evidence does indeed suggest that the great masters did intend to tune the plates to produce a vibrational frequency of 256Hz (middle C) from the sound holes. He goes on to say in the interview that "the sound comes back at you". Meaning of course that he could distinguish each of the individual tonal resonances of the chromatic scale as he proceeded up an octave. In this way he could in turn assess the relative amplitude of each of the resonances (notes), in the scale, and thereby make some adjustment to the thickness, (taper), of the plates, and the height of the rib. Hence, in this way enabling him to even out the resonance amplitudes.

Donald blows a chromatic scale starting on middle C into the f-hole.

Fine finishing work in progress – a time consuming process

Tools in Donald Riddell's fiddle workshop. The majority of his tools if not all, were hand made. This need arose because there were none commercially available to buy.

Donald sourced his own wood with a preference for Bog Fir – a wood which has been submerged in peat for a considerable period and had leached out various impurities – though he also used other species and also wood which he bought from down south, e.g. even Alder and Laburnum.

Fiddle made from Laburnum wood

The finished Luburnum fiddle.

Blow torch, solvents, varnish and wood stains. Presumably these would not have looked out of place in a Master Cremonese violin-makers workshop.

This photograph appears to show a clutter of material and an instrument lying on a bed in his workshop? The provenance of the instrument shown is uncertain. (Courtesy IMAG).

Donald Riddell outside his workshop

Eventually however, the stairs to his workshop had to be closed off after a fall to prevent him going back up. There is a uniqueness to this timeless image of a creative man in his working environment.

Workshop door sign - trusting security as practised in the Highlands

in his day – people rarely locked their doors

Recalling his own past, Donald remembers his time spent in the house of Alexander Battan Grant at Tomnahurich Farm on the outskirts of Inverness, (available on the AmBaile web site).

"In his house, a room up-stair - nobody was allowed into it. Even I was never in there. He took everything down to his room and I'd spend the whole day with him assessing the relative qualities of fiddles. We'd have nine or ten fiddles down - including these Rondello's - and we'd compare them - he would play or I would play and we'd discuss the relative merits. He just brought down, sometimes the pieces, but you didn't get up to see him working at a bench. Och, I think he made, in his lifetime, perhaps sixty or seventy, which is quite a good output, because it takes about a hundred and fifty hours to make a fiddle. You'll not make it much quicker than that, if you're turning out decent, decently finished work".

This photograph shows Donald Riddell playing the Rondello, the round violin invented and made by Alexander Battan Grant.

This round violin, or Rondello, was said to have sounded as clear as the human voice singing.

This photograph shows Donald Riddell playing a Grant Rondello.

Donald Riddell at the front door of his croft playing the Rondello.

Donald being interviewed in his Croft

Donald inspecting a violin made by Sandy Battan's

great grandson Michael Kerr at Clunes Croft (7-10-1990).

The above photo, and the following three, were taken from a video made by Alison Wilky for the BBC on the topic of violins in an interview with Donald in 1990. The video goes on to show Donald being interviewed by the noted Loch Ness monster hunter Dr Robert Rines at Clunes Croft.

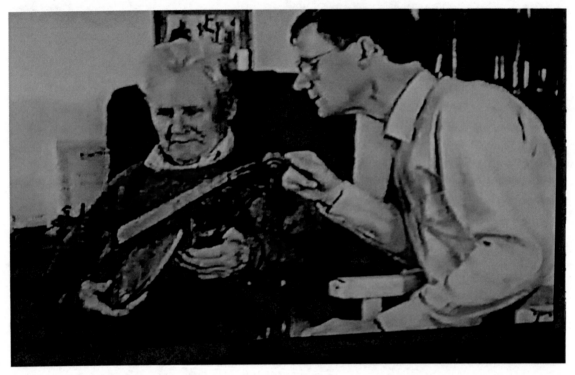

Donald produced from a cardboard box brought down from his bedroom the frame and parts of a Battan Grant Rondello – he presents a critique on the instrument in the video.

(Courtesy the BBC)

Dr Robert Rines, (Nessi Hunter and noted Polymath), interviews Donald at Clunes Croft in 1990.

(Notice the gun cabinet in the background referred to by Duncan Chisholm, in Part 4)

This interview recorded for the BBC in 1990 gives an interesting insight into Donald's view of traditional fiddle playing, and his fame as a teacher. In it Rines says 'I will sit at your feet as your pupil to learn how to do it'.

Donald and Bob, who was living close by at Tychat, overlooking Loch Ness and Urquhart Castle, went on to discuss Scottish fiddling and the differences between classical interpretation and traditional fiddling – with Donald saying that "classical musicians are more or less useless at it". Then they both laugh. A comment taken kindly By Rines.

Donald teaches Dr Robert Rines how to perform the Strathspey 'Snap'

and 'Arrow' bow strokes.

Dr Robert Rines, had in fact at the age of eleven years, played a violin duet with Albert Einstein at a summer camp in Main, USA – he said he played better than Einstein. Presumably, the claim that he had been taught to play traditional Snap and Arrow bow strokes by the 'Einstein of Traditional fiddling tuition' Donald Riddell, would make a worthy addition to his Curriculum Vitae also.

Donald also has a similar claim to fame when he met the International classical violin virtuosi Yehudi Menuhin at Blair Castle - but the general consensus was that Yehudi could not do it. However, Yehudi went on to invite Donald backstage at his concert being held at Eden Court, Inverness some time later. Testament indeed to this man from a humble croft of his skills, ability and fame. (A young Duncan Chisholm was taken to meet Menuhin and found him polite but remote).

[Donald had an interesting method for teaching young pupils. He would write out the tune to be played - right in front of the pupil - with all bowing carefully marked out. The pupil had the written music as a guide but learnt the tune by *watching* and *listening* to Donald carefully bowing it out. The pupil was expected to learn the tune by heart and play it *correctly* by the next lesson - otherwise no new tune – Duncan Chisholm, Part 4].

In his later years, Donald would occasionaly be taken to hear the Inverness Strathspey and Reel Society members play. It must have given him great joy to hear pupils, some of whom he may have taught, and be able to listen to this emergence of a new generation of youngsters who would carry on the tradition of Scottish fiddle playing which ment so much to him. The delight and joy in his eyes is clear to be seen in the video.

Truly proof of Battan Grant's legacy and Donald's continued contribution to the development of Highland Traditional Fiddle music.

Wheel chair enabled, Donald visits an IS&RS prctice session in Inverness.

Like his mentor, Alexander Grant, Donald restricted the Society's repertoire to a fixed number of sets, adding to the list only occasionally. Players became very familiar with the music and knew how to play it fluently. Years later, when members of the Society meet up, they unerringly play the 'old' tunes with exactly the same bowing and vigour as when they played under Donald's command.

As a young man, Donald had qualified as an Associate of the Tonic Solfa College of London and, as a music teacher, taught the violin in Skye and Oban before WW2. In his lifetime, he composed many fine fiddle and bagpipe tunes. In 1986, one of his former adult pupils, Mrs

Jean Cameron, managed for posterity to get Donald to publish the best of his own notable collection of bagpipe and fiddle compositions, 'The Clunes Collection of Scots Fiddle Music'.

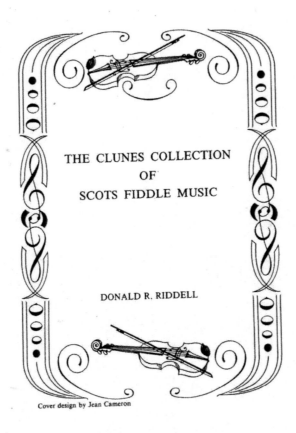

Donald's Music Book
(Courtesy Mrs Jean Cameron)

Two of the tunes need special mention: "Seoras Begg" (Wee Geordie) composed for his son; and "The Lament for King George V". The first is a six part tune that must rank with the best hornpipes ever composed, while the second is notable for its mood and inventiveness. The result is the preservation of yet another important slice of Scotland's heritage which might otherwise have been lost.

Many of the young pupils he taught enjoyed much success at competitions throughout Scotland and went on to make a name for themselves as professional musicians, with some achieving the status of International performers. The range of backgrounds of the pupils he taught was varied, and included that of Scottish aristocratic nobility.

**A painting of the late Hon. Hugh Alastair Joseph Fraser as a young boy
holding a half size fiddle made by Donald Riddell**
(Hugh was the 5th child of the 15th Lord Lovat of WW2 Normandy Landing fame. The painting hangs in
Balblair House - Dower house of Beauly Castle and Estate. Courtesy of Hugh's wife, Drusilla Fraser, and
family)
(© Sinclair Gair)

Balblair House where 'Shimi' Lovat, 15th Lord Lovat, lived during the latter years of his life.

(Courtesy of Hugh's wife, Drusilla Fraser, and family)

(© Sinclair Gair)

Donald Riddell's Time as a Pipe Major in the Lovat Scouts

A Lovat Scout Piper in Marching order

(Taken from March Past, a Memoir by Lord Lovat, Courtesy of the 16th Lord Lovat)

The Clan Fraser of Lovat's Role in Raising the Regiment (a brief background)

In the Middle Ages, the Frasers had acquired rich lands around the Valliscaulin priory of Beauly. These Frasers consolidated their territory, gradually spreading westwards into the glens of Inverness-shire, and embracing Gaeldom as they did so. Before long, a large clan formed round them and they in turn adopted the language and ethos of their Celtic neighbours. They continued by intermarrying or fighting with other clans until their lands stretched from the east to the west coasts of Scotland. Their chief was always and still is called Simon.

In 1737 the Simon Lovat who became known to the English as the 'Old (Red) Fox' was one of the first clan chiefs to join the Association of Jacobite Support, which backed the exiled King James. From the safety of Rome, James had made him Lord Lovat of Beauly, Viscount of the Aird and Strathglass, Earl of Stratherrick and Abertarff, Marquis of Beaufort and Duke of Fraser – [and as Veronica Maclean, daughter of the 14th Lord Lovat notes in her book 'Past Forgetting' - quite enough for an upwardly mobile Highlander to be getting on with!].

However, in 1745 the Old Fox found he had backed the wrong side (despite trying to back both), and after the Prince's defeat at Culloden, he fled to loch Morar, was captured by the Duke of Cumberland's Redcoats, imprisoned, and in 1747 beheaded on Tower Hill. It is said that on the morning of his execution a large scaffolding structure was built to accommodate

211

a part of the considerable crowd which had gathered. Built in a rush, or simply over-loaded, the temporary seating collapsed crushing many and killing five or six people. Standing on the gallows platform, the Old Fox (at eighty years of age), burst out laughing – hence the origin of the expression 'laughing your head off' – apocryphal or true? Quoting again from Veronica's book….the library at Beaufort was a typical eighteenth century collection of rather dull classical and religious books. Dotted around the house were one or two quite decent pictures, 'as well as Simon Lovat of the '45's false teeth and spectacles, in a glass case' – surely a talking point for any visitors.

In recent times, as of now, his 'supposed' lead coffin was opened in the Wardlaw Mausoleum, at Kirkhill Cemetery, in order to substantiate the rumour that some Jacobite supporters had spirited his body away after the execution and returned it to Scotland. However, this story was quashed once and for all when the contents were revealed to be a mixture of bones, some of which were identified as belonging to a young girl. So, the likely hood is that he was indeed buried at Tower Hill.

Instead of getting the Dukedom (promised again by Bonnie Prince Charlie), and the magnificent new castle for which William Adam had drawn up plans, the Lovat family saw their lands sequestrated, and Castle Downie (or Beaufort, as it was later called), which had been sacked and burnt in 1745, steadily crumbled into ruin. They retained only one nearby smaller castle - Monaick – which had survived both the '15 and the '45. Eventually, the Lovat attainder to the United Kingdom barony was not raised until 1857 – and then only at Queen Victoria's express wish.

Lovat's Scouts: The following excerpt is quoted from 'The Story of the Lovat Scouts, 1900 – 1980', by Michael Leslie Melville. (Courtesy of his family).

"Founded by Simon the 14th Lord Lovat and twenty-second Chief of the Clan Fraser of Lovat, raised the Lovat Scouts early in the year 1900 to fight in the South African Boer War - 'A Chief among his own people and leader of a thousand warriors'. The family name in Gaelic has been MacShimidh (the son of Simon) from time immemorial.

Beaufort Castle (Lord Lovat), Beauly

Beauly Castle, the family home of the Frasers of Lovat. The right hand part of the building was destroyed by fire during 1935.

Simon Joseph was brought up at Beaufort Castle, the family home near Beauly in Inverness-shire. The earliest mention of the site, as Downie or Dounie castle, occurs in the reign of Alexander 1, (1106 – 1224) of Scotland. The regiment, based upon individual merit, allowed for every idiosyncrasy, and was held together by an intrinsic discipline more reminiscent of the Shinty field than the parade ground, with bonds of friendship rather than of hierarchy between men and officers. This never quite fitted into any Whitehall or War Office pattern or design.

Beauly Castle, ancestral home of the Lords of Lovat, sits above

the Beauly river, near the small town of Beauly in the Scottish Highlands.
(Taken from March Past, a Memoir by Lord Lovat, Courtesy of the current 16th Lord Lovat)

The Scouts were raised initially and swiftly from across the highland glens and estates (the Fraser estates extended to more than 250,000 acres at that time). Mainly drawn from estate workers, stalkers and gillies with their in-bred ability to shoot and use a spy glass – they were an essential element for war reconnaissance at which they excelled.

The Lovat Scouts in camp beneath Beauly Castle 1910 – note their horses interspersed throughout the camp.

The same spot – more or less as it is today in 2020

Initially the Scouts were a mounted unit – Beauly Square in the background.

The Scouts were a family Regiment in more ways than one. In 1939 for example, there were approximately 100, including eleven officers, who were sons of former Scouts. Each Squadron teemed with brothers, uncles, nephews, and cousins. In A Squadron for example there were four sons of Sgt. Duncan Fraser, head stalker at Braulen, and in the Ross-shire Troop there were four Ross brothers, all in the same Section. About a score of officers were to have served in the Scouts who were related by blood or by marriage to Colonel Archie Stirling, whose mother had been a Leslie Melville, and who had married Lord Lovat' sister. In some Troops a great many of the local men were of the same clan surname, and so were called by their Christian names, nicknames or numbers.

However, some rough edges in congealing as a coherent fighting force led Lord Lovat (14th) at one time to write in a letter. 'The great difficulty of the new hands was in recognising their horses after they had off-saddled and been turned out. There were conversations such as: 'He's my horse'; No, it's my y'en'; 'Gosh man, but it's awfu' like me ane'; 'Gie's a look'; 'I had a bit string on mine'. Or on another occasion - on starting the day hurriedly, I spotted a rifleman mounting his horse without his gun. "Where's your rifle?" "Dash it, I clean forgot her!"…

On his return from South Africa, the 14th Lord Lovat was awarded the military C.B. for his achievements in the campaign. There was a civic function in his honour in Inverness and the Lovat tenantry and feuars of The Aird and Fort Augustus raised £500 with which they wished to present Lord Lovat with his portrait. He suggested, instead, that it should be spent on a memorial to the Scouts and, in particular, to those who fell in the Boer War. It was completed in 1905 and unveiled by Mackintosh of Mackintosh, Lord Lieutenant of Inverness-shire. Of simple design and nearly fifty feet high, it stands in the centre of the square in Beauly and is suitably inscribed".

The square in Beauly with the newly erected (1905) Lovat Scout monument

Lovat Scouts Memorial, Beauly, in honour of the Scouts who fell in the Boer War. Erected by the 14th Lord Lovat, Simon Joseph Fraser, Baron Lovat (He was legally the 14th, but styled himself 16th due to the fact that the family was proscribed after the Jacobite Rebellion in 1745).

(© Sinclair Gair)

SIMON JOSEPH, 16th LORD LOVAT,
KT., G.C.V.O., K.C.M.G., C.B., D.S.O.
1932

With the Boer war years behind him, Lord Lovat became the first Chairman of the Forestry Commission. He was succeeded in 1933 by his son and heir, Simon Christopher Joseph Fraser, Master of Lovat and 15th Lord Lovat.

In turn, Shimi Lovat, 15th, went on to become a Major in the Lovat Scouts, and was later appointed Brigadier of 4 Commando, following the WW2 Normandy landings on Sword Beach, and the successful holding of the bridges over the Caen Canal and the River Orne.

The 15th Lord Lovat's first son and heir Simon Augustine Fraser, Master of Lovat, and his fourth son Andrew Fraser predeceased him in 1994 within days of each other. The 15th Lord Lovat then died a year later in 1995. The title has now passed to his grandson Simon Christopher Fraser who is the current 16th Lord Lovat.

Queen Elizabeth and Prince Philip accompanied by Lord Lovat (15th),

center, stand beneath the Lovat Monument in Beauly Square, July 10th, 1981.

Donald's Piping Career

By the time he joined the Lovat Scouts at the beginning of the 2nd World War, Donald was a connoisseur of piping.

Donald Riddell standing on the right hand side

Donald learnt to play the bagpipes from Pipe Major William Young. He played for 8 years in the territorial band of the Cameron Highlanders and was also Pipe Major of the Wardlaw Band in Kiltarlity.

He was soon selected as pipe major of the band and qualified as pipe major at the Edinburgh Castle school run by the legendary Pipe Major Willie Ross in a record 3 days. His service took him to the Faroes, Canada, Italy and Greece. The regiment had a number of talented pipers – most of them from the Outer Hebrides - whom Donald moulded into a very fine band which easily won the Scottish Command Pipe Band competition in 1942. The band went on to make many notable public performances.

**Lovat Scouts Pipe Band Marching in the Faroes during their
two year war posting, with Donald leading at the head (front row right).**

After the war, Donald returned home and settled at South Clunes, near Kirkhill, Inverness-shire. He devoted his time to crofting, music and making violins.

(The following is quoted from 'The Story of the Lovat Scouts, 1900 – 1980', by Michael Leslie Melville. Courtesy of his family).

"The pipe band was always the pride and glory of the Lovat Scouts. From 1922 onwards, an exceptionally fine Pipe Band was gradually built up largely thanks to the late Lt. Colonel J.P. Grant of Rothiemurchus, himself a great authority on piping, who recruited for many years the very best of young pipers from the Islands, particularly South Uist. For twelve years the famous Pipe Major Willie Ross (formerly of the Scots Guards) was in charge of the Scout's Band, and he was succeeded by several other outstanding Pipe Majors, notably, Lt Colonel Dick Allhusen, who devoted himself to the task.

Donald Riddell, who was then a N.C.O. in A Squadron but had been a piper in the Camerons and also Pipe Major to the Wardlaw Pipe Band near Kiltarlity, was made Pipe Major. He proved to be the ideal person for the job. He was a splendid leader, who insisted on the highest standard of smartness and military efficiency, as well as being a gifted musician and connoisseur of piping.

In the summer of 1942, the Scouts won the Scottish Command Pipe Band Competition by a very wide margin. At Balmoral they played superbly both years. In the spring of 1943, they broadcast from Glasgow, and Pipe Major Riddell recalls that it was the first occasion the public had heard an entire Pipe Band playing jigs together. It amazed even the city of Glasgow Police Pipers!

**The Lovat Scouts with Donald Riddell at the head (front row right)
perform guard duty for the Queen at Balmoral Castle in 1942.**

**The Lovat Scouts with Donald Riddlell (left hand side, standing)
perform guard duty for the Queen at Balmoral Castle in 1943.**
(The photo shows the Royal Family at Balmoral with Senior N.C.O.s and
Lt. Col. A. Fairrie, M.B.E., Major Dickson and Captain W. Gammell, Adjutant)

In Vancouver they gave two performances which are remembered to this this day, in Aquila they played to several thousand Italians and, after the war, they joined with the Scottish Horse Pipe Band to play to a huge crowd in Kiagenfurt, which received much publicity.

On each day, the designated Orderly Piper from the band played 'Hey, Jonny Cope' for Reveille, 'Brose and Butter' for each meal, and for On Parade, 'Inveresk House'. Each evening except in Italy, he played for the Officers Mess – usually two 'Sets', some jigs and a piobaireachd.

The Regimental March is, of course Morair Sim (Lord Simon). This great tune is believed to date from about 1715, but was first published in 1874, then written as a Strathspey, by Captain Fraser of Knockie.

Donald Riddell's arrangement and hand written version of Morair Sim, (Lord Simon), the Lovat Scouts Regimental March.

The Scouts at Weybourne camp 1955, Donald standing front row right.

'The Lovat Scouts', never used as the Regimental March, was written by Scott Skinner ('Talent does what it can: genius does what it must') about 1900 as a fiddle tune. [author's note - I have played this tune at the start of a Gay Gordons set at many ceilidh dances in castles, stately homes and posh Hotels e.g. Gleneagles Hotel, on many occasions]. For ceremonial occasion each Squadron had its own slow march: 'Sons of Glencoe' (A Sqn.), 'The Mist Covered Mountains' (B Sqn.), 'The Hawk That Swoops On High' (C Sqn), and 'Mo Dhachaidh' (D Sqn.).

In Italy the pipe band played an important role. As well as providing guards for Regimental Head Quarters, they were frequently used throughout the campaign as stretcher bearers, which was no light task, especially in hill country, and often a very dangerous one. Two of them were killed and one wounded in gallantly endeavouring to rescue the wounded from mine fields.

During the first World War whilst fighting in Macedonia, (October 1916 – 1918), the Scouts found themselves up against the Bulgars, who had taken over from the Turks. In an engagement that overall came to be known as the Salma affair, the Scouts successfully ambushed a Bulgar patrol and in the process relieved them of a set of bagpipes. They were so dirty and disgusting that not one Scout would attempt to play them".

Lovat Scouts in the Second World War had good reason to be proud of their brilliant pipe band.

Having served as Pipe Major of the Lovat Scouts throughout the war, Donald was given a special mention by Lord Lovat in his book 'March Past'.

[Lord Lovat, (cousin of David Stirling founder of the SAS), led 4 Commando (whom he had helped establish in the Scottish Highlands), and led the unit at Sword Beach during the Normandy D-Day landings.

15th Lord Lovat - a Lovat Scout Officer and subsequently Brigadier of 4 Commando, Normandy Landings, Sword Beach, World War 2.

(Taken from March Past, a Memoir by Lord Lovat, Courtesy of the 16th Lord Lovat)

15th Lord Lovat in Military Uniform

(Taken from March Past, a Memoir by Lord Lovat, Courtesy of the 16th Lord Lovat)

Lord Lovat was later badly wounded out of the Army when the unit encountered determined opposition in their successful attempt to hold the bridges over the River Orne, and the Caen Canal. In his retirement from the army, Lovat had this to say about Donald Riddell and the Lovat Scouts:

"Dick Allhusen took the musicians in hand. Donald Riddell – a capable crofter on the Lovat Estate lands, who in his spare time makes cabinets and violins – was promoted to pipe-major and sent on a drill course, followed by a visit to the Army School of Piping on the Castle Rock in Edinburgh. The Scouts were subsequently posted for two years of exile in the Faroes – which worked wonders with the band. The Western Isles pipers (ten of them came from South Uist), steeped in knowledge of the bagpipe (its music, virtuosity and fingering in which they excelled), had all started army life as individual players. Islanders hold a poor opinion of noisy accompaniment and the thump of kettle-drums. Conventional march tunes (which most bands play) they consider fit only for children and beginners. They did not find it easy to counter-march or keep in step.

The piping could not be improved, but the drill and turnout were transformed. The reputation of the band went before them to Vancouver. While the regiment was training in the Rockies, the City Fathers, by general request, sent an invitation to Jasper Park: 'Please come and play at City Hall!'. The performance was an unqualified success, for the vast dominion of Canada is Scotland writ large across a continent. That day every Highlander on the Pacific Coast was at the station, with his family and a bottle of whisky, to welcome the visitors. Most pipers have 'hollow legs', but all records were broken on this occasion. If the pipes and drums marched away in good order to 'The Black Bear' – a compliment to their hosts – another tune, 'The Big Spree', was certainly more appropriate".]

Royal Recognition

Out of all the well-known and accomplished violinists/fiddlers in the country that could have been selected, Donald was the one chosen to play at the funeral of King George the 5th in London. On his return home Donald, sufficiently moved by the occasion, composed a lament for the King titled, "The Lament for King George V". A deeply notable piece which is contained in his book of tunes 'The Clunes Collection of Scots Fiddle Music'.

**Donald receiveing his Britiah Empire Medal (BEM) from the Queen
for services to violin teaching and playing.**

In 1988, Donald was awarded the British Empire Medal by the Queen for services to Scottish traditional fiddling.

A skilled man who had to make his own workshop tools because they

could not be sourced or bought. He made splendid instruments

in this unassuming workshop above his pig sty.

His upstairs workshop eventually became out of bounds even to him following a fall whilst descending the outside access stairs in his elderly years.

Donald in his latter years (1990) – a life well lived which he shared generously with others and thereby helped improve theirs.

Donald's final farewell:

Guest – I look forward to my next visit;

Donald – Aye, that would be grand,

.....all the best.

Time passes and dreams float away with distant

memories of a great traditional fiddle player, teacher, and Lovat Scout Pipe Major now gone.

(Donald passed away in 1992)

Donald lies burried (small stone), close to the Lovat Mausoleum, in Wardlaw Cemetery, Kirkhill, near Beauly.

(© Sinclair Gair)

Direction sign on main road running through Kirkhill.

(© Sinclair Gair)

It is to be hoped that he, like Grant, will never be forgotten and people will make the effort to remember him by visiting the area in the Scottish Highlands in which he spent most of his life.

A Sandy Battan Grant Violin rests on a lenght of Lovat Fraser tartan – soon to be made into Donald Frasers Kilt, Morisons Ironmongers, Beauly. (Note: we know that he is/was known Internationally but doubt that Battan held European and British passports – did you notice up till now?......Laura Fraser!!).

Part 4

Todays Modern Heritage – A Tribute by Bruce MacGregor/ Duncan Chisholm - the Grant/Riddell standard bearers, as of 2019.

Donald Riddell (1909 - 1992)

Grant's Musical Heritage – continued through Donald Riddell.

In turn, Donald Riddell's teaching and fiddle playing heritage has been passed on today through his many pupils, notably Duncan Chisholm, and Bruce MacGregor - the list is extensive and it has been a worthwhile experience to have met a few of them.

An Overview

(The following extract from an interview given by Duncan Chisholm is taken from the Inverness Courier, 2009).

The 16th annual Celtic Connections Music Festival, Glasgow. Among the artists making the journey down the A9 will be two of Scotland's leading fiddle players Duncan Chisholm and Bruce MacGregor. They, together with MacGregor's Blazin Fiddles bandmate Iain MacFarlane from Glenfinnan, will be paying tribute to their fiddle teacher Donald Riddell, who farmed at South Clunes seven miles west of Inverness. The three fiddlers have already recorded a tribute to their old teacher in the album "A Highland Fiddler", but the album was predated by a couple of live shows for the Highland Festival. Now "A Highland Fiddler" is making its Glasgow debut at St Andrew's in the Square in just over a week on Saturday 24th January and is already a sell out.

Blazin Fiddles – led by Bruce MacGregor (2nd left).

"The one thing we would say we all got from Donald was a pretty good idea of technique", said Chisholm, who was a pupil of Riddell for eight years. He wasn't a very strict man, he was a very caring teacher, but you had to do it his way up until the point when he decided to let you fly the nest. I remember him saying: "You've spent the last eight years playing like Donald Riddell. Now you've got to go and play like Duncan Chisholm".

Riddell died in 1992, by which time Chisholm was already making a name for himself with the Celtic rock band Wolfstone. Chisholm does not know if his former mentor ever heard Wolfstone, but, does not think Riddell would not have disapproved of his pupil's new direction.

"Ultimately he was a musical man and I'm sure he would have seen it as a step forward for the music. Although he was a strict disciplinarian about the music, he had a very open mind as well". Chisholm added.

Many more of Riddell's former pupils continue to play, demonstrating his continuing influence on fiddle playing in the Highlands and beyond. Chisholm calculates that Riddell was seeing around 50 students a week when he was a pupil.

One important aspect of Riddell's teaching, Chisholm believes, was that his music was grounded in the traditions of both west and east Scotland.

Though he appreciates the grounding in the fiddle technique that learning the Scott Skinner repertoire of strathspeys and reels gave him, Chisholm confessed: "I was always more into the pipe marches and Gaelic airs. That meant more to me than the tunes of Scott Skinner, but I was lucky to get both of them in the teaching".

Another plus for Chisholm about next weekend's concert is that unlike most of his other musical outlets, it allows him to play along with fellow fiddlers. "I can play with Bruce and Iain and get totally different things from playing with either of them", he said. "I just love playing with both of them and it's always a pleasure".

(i) A Tribute from Bruce MacGregor

I was very lucky to be taught the fiddle by one of Scotland's greatest, Donald Riddell, without whom I would'nt have played a note. I can hear his voice clearly, and I can still see those massive, bushy, white eyebrows raising in amazement/disappointment at my musical scratching. Donald was a Pipe Major in the Lovat Scouts, a classical violinist, a Scottish fiddler, a story teller, a Gaelic and Welsh speaker, a cabinet maker and a fiddle maker. He was inspirational to so many and he left many great memories.

I vividly remember being transfixed to the cigarette hanging off his lips during our lessons, freely dripping ash over his newly crafted fiddle's, most without even a lick of varnish at that stage. I remember the pigs running in and out of his croft, the escaped pet hedgehog, the cats everywhere and the first time ever going to toilet and discovering ripped up newspaper instead of Andrex, (a modern – at the time - toilet utility paper).

I remember a lot about that great man. What I really appreciate today are the stories he told me about the tunes; the composers, the places that inspired the music. For Donald, traditional music needed context. A tune is just a series of notes in a format, and no matter the amazing technical dexterity of a musician, the melody will always just be this collection of notes until it has context. It does'nt have to be a hilarious anecdote, it can just be a mental image that connects the listener to the tune, a place, a person, a description.

The scene which would have greeted Bruce when he first arrived at Clunes for his music lessons with Donald – in addition to other forms of wildlife.

My grasp on music theory is really poor and it was one thing I glossed over with Donald. I remember him asking me to read the key signature of a new tune he'd put up in front of me. I'd squint at it, have a guess, and because of the nature of Scottish music (most tunes are in A, D or G) I had a one-in-three chance of getting it right!

I learnt more from listening to him play the tunes rather than reading the manuscript. Learning by ear was a technique he actively encouraged. It gave you freedom from the page and it let you feel the music better. It also helped develop skills for improvising and adding variations for tunes, both vital for the continuing development of Scottish music.

I remember getting my fiddle for my seventh Christmas. I honestly do'nt remember asking for it! I also could'nt work out how to get a sound out of the thing as neither myself or my parents had any idea what rosin was, nor indeed how to tighten the bow! It was a half-size Chinese instrument that produced a sound so painful only parents could really listen to it. I certainly did'nt get over excited about it at the time, there were toy guns with laser lights to play with.

It must have been a few weeks later I was taken to Donald Riddell for an initial meeting. It was quite a distance out of town and in-fact it was so remote that we had to do the last bit to his croft on foot through deep snow. I was there for about two minutes. Donald looked me up and down and gave me a gruff hello then turned to my father and said "Too wee. Take him back in a year". That was it. I'm pretty certain I wasn't that bothered.

Memories of my first lessons are as clear as day. I was taught the "anatomy" of the fiddle along with the string names. The first tune I played was "There is a happy land". What still amazes me about Donald's teaching was that he moved you on so quickly, without going through years of scales or theory. He was a fully qualified music teacher, but for him getting kids excited about Scottish music was much more important at this stage in our development. I moved on from the Skye Boat Song to The Piper Weird, The Earl of Mansfield and The Bluebells of Scotland. Donald would sit there and hand write the tunes in seconds. An amazing skill he perfected when Pipe Major of the Lovat Scouts, long before the age of photocopiers.

The music was then put up in front of me with the finger numbers and string name written above (so a high F would be E1). The bowing was also clearly marked and HAD to be adhered to, if not, you were back to the beginning. There was no time limit to classes. If you were playing well and receptive then the lesson continued, despite others coming in for their lessons. They just had to wait. As I've grown older I realized that this wan't Donald having no concern for time. He was after all a Pipe Major where timing was pretty vital! I'm convinced it was his way of inspiring other kids. In the lead-up to competitions he was a devil for saying "Aye, not bad. You should hear how Duncan Chisholm/Mathew Finlayson/Rory MacLeod is playing that tune. Ver good". It was his way of saying practice more!

Every week a new tune was presented to me, normally something more challenging. If you did'nt hit the required standard he would say "Aye, a bit sticky" which considering what my granny was giving me afterwards seemed about right!

The tunes of master fiddlers Neil Gow, Simon Fraser and James Scott Skinner were introduced alongside the great piping repertoire of GS MacLennan and Peter MacLeod. These tunes sat alongside the songs of the Highland Gaels and were mixed with stories about the composers and the lands they were from, and also the reasoning behind the tune titles. Sometimes we were told stories about his days in the army, in Italy and Canada or his teaching in Skye. The history and story telling were almost as important as the music itself.

To progress to the ranks of the Highland Strathspey and Reel Society, the group which Donald led after reforming the group in 1972, you had to memorise the music. Lots of music! Before playing to a public audience, you were expected to know three hours-worth of material by memory – NO SHEET MUSIC ALLOWED!

The notes were one thing, but Donald insisted that EVERY bowing had to be the same within the group. You can imagine the influence of having a former Pipe Major as your fiddle teacher might have! It was hard, but ultimately rewarding discipline, and one that has served so many of his pupils to this day. One incident sticks in my mind which shows the power of his tuition. I met up with Duncan Chisholm, years after we'd both been taught by Donald, for a session. We fired into a jig that we had picked up independently (I think is was Rory MacLeod) and I watched in amazement as our bowing synched up, stroke by stroke.

Donald always said that you could develop your own sound and style, but it was very clear that whilst he gave you this aspiration, when he was teaching you, it was "his way". On reflection I am so glad of that discipline. He gave us the voice and now we have the opportunity of articulating and expressing our emotions through music; an incredible gift.

He made me very conscious of our Highland voice and our distinct culture and that is something we have continued the work of through Blazin Fiddles. The band was set up in 1998 when I became disillusioned with much of the output on our national broadcaster, BBC Radio Scotland. I worked there as a producer and the music I heard on peak time afternoon shows was predominantly Irish and Cape Breton. Scottish fiddling was restricted to Aly Bain and maybe a bit of Alasdair Fraser. There was one incident in America that really kicked me into action. I was attending the Valley of the Moon Scottish Fiddle School in California, making a documentary for the BBC about this incredible event in the Redwood Forest.

I asked one elderly gent what he knew of Scottish fiddle music today. His answer was "Well, its dead isn't it. There aren't any youngsters playing and the music is probably more alive here in California than it is in Scotland".

I mentioned to him a few names; Duncan Chisholm, Iain MacFarlane, Allan Henderson. He Hadn't heard of any of them and I realised that as usual with the Scots, and particularly the Highlanders, we had just failed to market and promote our great young musicians. I looked to Ireland and Cape Breton and what I saw was fine players but with superb media and promotion behind them.

That's where the spark for Blazin' Fiddles came from, it was a chip on my shoulder, a desire to shout "Hey world, listen to this. This is Scotland". The band was formed to showcase the regional voices in the Highlands and Islands and that core message has remained to this day – the sounds of Shetland, Orkney, Inverness and the west coast. We've played everywhere from Buckingham Palace to the Royal Albert Hall to Plockton Village Hall. From packed arenas in Cape Breton to Glastonbury Festival and to village gatherings but always the message is the same – this is the music of the Highlands and Islands. We are so proud to carry on the music of Willie Hunter, Aonghas Grant and of course Donald Riddell and hope that in some way the music we play will inspire the next generation to continue this incredible heritage we have.

Blazin in Beauly

This annual work shop has been organized and run by Bruce MacGregor for the last 20 years. It has continued the teaching tradition set by Donald Riddle of providing traditional fiddle tuition to multiple participants - not only from the Highlands, but from all over Scotland and further afield. The event is held in the Lovat Hotel, and in order to accommodate all of the participants in other venues in Beauly also. It is entirely fitting that one of the venues is held in Morisons Ironmongers shop – immediately across the road from the Lovat, and of course the shop once owned by Donald Morison assistant to Battan Grant in the early days of the Highland Strathspey and Reel Society – started over one hundred years ago. Grant and Skinner were frequent visitors to Morison for the enjoyment and pleasure of playing together.

Some of the attendee's at a Blazin in Beauly Workshop held in the Lovat Arms Hotel

The scope of the tuition undertaken is complemented by well known folk performers who are ready to share their skills and to pass on their individual experiences for the benefit of a new generation of players. Donald Riddell, were he alive today, would have undoubtedly been immensely proud of Bruce's efforts, and success, in continuing his teaching tradition which was passed on to him by Alexander Battan Grant.

A group fiddle teaching session in the Lovat Hotel 2018

Battan Grant's Rondello Makes a Return Visit to Inverness

One of the unique disc shaped violin instruments made by Alexander 'Battan' Grant over one hundred years ago was brought back to Inverness by his great grandson Michael Kerr. Apart from the one held in the Inverness Museum and Art Gallery, this instrument is the sole remaining example of Grant's supreme violin making skills. This photo shoot for the Inverness

Courier was held in MacGregors Bar, Academy Street, Inverness on the 14th December 2019. The premises are at the opposite end of Academy Street from where Grant opened his Fishing tackle makers business in 7 Baron Taylor Lane (now Street) in 1888.

Bruce holds the treasured instrument and

admires Grant's exquisite workmanship

(© Sinclair Gair)

Bruce MacGregor, Donald Fraser and Michael Kerr with the Rondello
and Michael's own hand crafted violin.
(Under the stylised watchful eye of Bruce's old former clan chief, the infamous – and
presumably well loved - Rob Roy MacGregor).

(© Sinclair Gair)

And as be-fits the occasion:

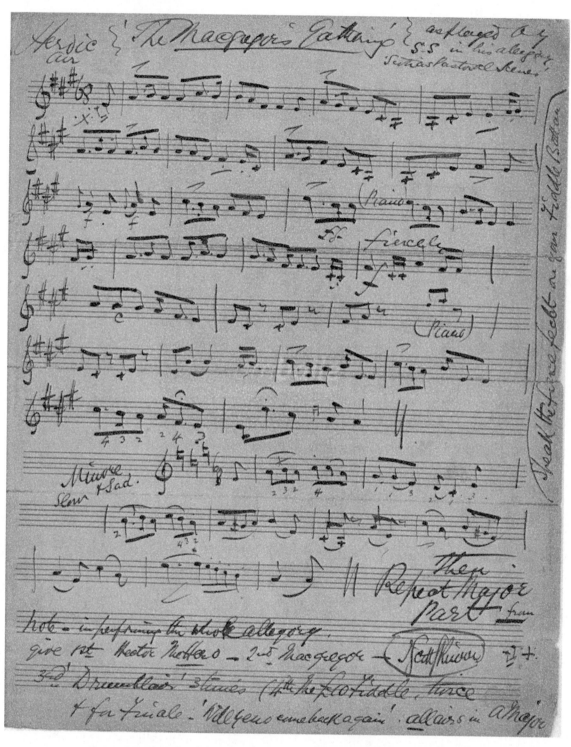

Arrangement for 'The Macgregors' Gathering' by Scott Skinner.

This hand-written manuscript (undated) was sent to Grant from Skinner. It contains an arrangement by Scott Skinner for the heroic air, 'The Macgregors' Gathering'.

(ii) An appreciation from Duncan Chisholm

Before travelling to Australia in April 2019 for a two month long musical tour, Duncan provided the following well penned tribute to his teacher – he makes clear from his writing the strength of the bond and fondness he had for his teacher.

Duncan in Concert

My first memory of Donald Riddell was when I was seven years old. I was taken by my parents to a concert in the local village hall at Inchmore near Kirkhill.

What I remember very clearly from that night was a very resplendent man with grey hair, very smartly dressed in a kilt, standing with his back to the audience playing the fiddle. He was leading the Highland Strathspey and Reel Society who were the main attraction for the evening. I would have thought there would have been about 12 players on the stage and the sound absolutely captivated me. I had never heard anything like it before. The tunes were played with military precision, all fiddle bows synchronised in spectacular fashion. This was a special moment for me, and I was hooked immediately.

My parents could obviously see that I had been clearly taken with the sound of the fiddle and so they asked me if I would like to take fiddle lessons with Donald as he only lived a matter of four miles from Kirkhill. I said yes on the spot and so they approached him after the concert. He asked my father how old I was, and my father said I was seven. Donald replied by saying that he was sorry, but I wasn't old enough and he wouldn't take me until my eighth birthday which wasn't until the end of October......and this was only June!!!!

In retrospect this stalling until I was 'old enough' to take lessons just fired me up more and my enthusiasm for the fiddle grew throughout those intervening months. So, at the start of November 1976 I went to South Clunes for my first lesson with the great Donald Riddell.

Duncan at Clunes taking part in an early television broadcast

in 1990 of 'Weir's Way'

The lesson started with Donald taking a fiddle case off the top of a sideboard and presenting me with it. The case was wooden and shaped like a coffin and inside sat a 3/4 size fiddle and bow. I couldn't believe it, my very own fiddle and my very own bow. This first lesson consisted of Donald systematically going through all the various parts of the fiddle. The bridge, the ribs, the f-holes, the nut, the scroll, the bow, the frog, the sound-post, all new terminology that had to be learnt.

He told me that "next week we will start to play a tune, I'll teach you to read music and then you will learn to memorise it and play it without any music sheets……you never see the birds in the trees with music in front of them so you shouldn't have any either". The first tune he taught me was 'There is a happy land'….this was the first and last tune he ever taught me from out with the Scottish tradition. The second and third tunes were 'The Skye Boat Song' and 'The Bluebells of Scotland'.

Week by week I learnt the tunes by memory and if they weren't learnt they would be given back to me to learn the following week. There was to be no quarter given in terms of what was expected of me. I would learn the notes and learn the bowing absolutely as was dictated and if it wasn't right it was given back to me until it was right. He wrote the fingers I should be playing and the string I should be on and we took it from there. Within a couple of month's I didn't need the fingers written down and started to understand how music was written and how it was played correctly.

The master and his pupil – this unique image captures a moment in time as Scottish traditional fiddle music, stretching as far back as Niel Gow (1727), was being passed on to a younger generation (1990) - by way of Alexander Battan Grant, and now the late Donald Riddell, to Duncan Chisholm.

The synchronicity of bowing in the Highland Strathspey and Reel Society that had been so impressive at Inchmore Hall was down to Donald's unfailing dedication to the way he believed these tunes should be played. This was a military operation and there was no doubt it worked. The bowing of a fiddle is a very personal act, it more than anything else creates the sound that comes out of the instrument. It forges the personality of the music you play, and in many respects tells people who you are as a person and the way you feel emotionally. When Donald taught us to bow, he was basically teaching us the way that he bowed. This is all he could have done as when you are learning an instrument you require guidance until you start to think for yourself. Donald's bowing certainly sunk in, if you put Bruce MacGregor and myself in separate rooms now and gave us a new tune, I would hazard a guess that we would bow the tune 90% the same. This bowing technique certainly came from Alexander Grant, which in turn came from Scott Skinner. These two musicians were Donald's greatest influence outside of the Bagpipe tradition which he loved. Donald would tell of the first time he saw Scott Skinner at the Phipps Hall in Beauly. He cycled down to see him play and was obviously incredibly impressed by the man.

Skinner's tunes didn't really ever connect with me. He was a product of the Victorian Music Hall and I never felt an affinity with that music, music that I felt was technically advanced but for me not emotionally stimulating. What the Skinner tunes did provide however were study's in technique and as week by week, tune by tune we went through 'The Scottish Violinist' book my command of what I was doing vastly improved.

Donald's classes were taken in the old school hall in Kenneth street Inverness and latterly above the ice rink. A very young Duncan Chisholm is 2ⁿᵈ left, kneeling in the front row. Donald himself is seen standing on the right wearing a Lovat Fraser tartan kilt.

The fiddle is an instrument which evokes an accent in everyone who plays it. During the 1970's there were still very much localised styles throughout Scotland, something that has changed considerably over the last 40 years. A fiddle style back then would change from town to town and it was quite easy to spot where someone was from depending on how they played a tune, very much like someone's voice changed from place to place.

These days our 'musical voice' is not dependent upon where we are from but ultimately about who we are as people, how we react emotionally and what our character is like.

Donald's style of music was firmly rooted between the east coast and the west, exactly where he lived geographically. As such we learnt the east coast tunes of Skinner and the Pipe tunes that would be so associated with the West Highland style of fiddle playing.

I loved the pipe tunes that Donald would teach me. He had been a Pipe Major in the Lovat Scouts during WW2 and had a great knowledge of the Pipe Marches, Reels and Jigs that had come through the military.

He also would teach the tunes of Neil Gow, William Marshall and various Gaelic melodies which all were a joy to learn.

Donald had a great memory for stories and history. Our lessons would consist of him explaining the tune he was going to teach. He would talk about the composer, perhaps then he would explain where and when the tune was written and more often than not why it was written. He would colourfully describe the background to whatever tune he was teaching thus giving it a life and three dimensions to a piece of music. This conjured up visual images in me which still lie at the root of my inspiration when writing and performing.

Donald saw active service during the war in Italy. He would tell of being encircled in a building under fire in Italy for days waiting until reinforcements arrived and passing the time by designing the gun cabinet that sat in living room at Clunes (see photo in Part 4). He also spent time during the war in the Faroes and in Canada and wrote a number of tunes while in service. Grindaboo was a favourite of mine, a 6/8 march tune written in the Faroes when he was there. Grindaboo was the shout the locals would give when the whaling ships came in (I remember him saying translated it meant "The whales have come") He would tell of the sea being red with blood as the Faroese stripped the whales.

'GRINDEBO' Whale Hunt at Sando, 1941

Before the war Donald spent time in Portree teaching. I remember him telling of a minister who would preach about this 'disciple of the devil' teaching music in their midst. He was the only passenger on a bus once going to Portree and while stopped in Broadford the minister got on the bus. Seeing Donald at the back of the bus he sat on the front seat. Every so often he would look back and Donald would be one seat further forward each time.

Such was the man, someone not to be crossed, someone who rightly commanded respect. The Highland Strathspey and Reel Society of the 1970's was his creation. There had of course been a society in his younger years when Alex Grant was leader but the Society I knew was his creation and his pride. Players in the HSRS were taught by him and many played fiddles that were made by him. This was entirely his sound and that was truly a remarkable achievement. I had been learning fiddle for about a year before Donald invited me to join the society. By this time, I had learnt quite a number of the tunes required to sit in for weekly rehearsals and hopefully my bowing would be up to scratch to join the synchronised bowing of everyone else. These Society rehearsals would take place every Monday night in the draughty and cold Cathedral Hall in Inverness. Later it would move to the Kenneth Street Hall and then a room above the Ice Rink. Just before I joined the HSRS there had been a very acrimonious split in the Society when a number of players left. The disagreement was over

Donald's overall leadership and a demand for different tunes to be played other than the repertoire Donald put forward. The Inverness Fiddlers were borne out of this split and for years afterwards there would be two fiddle groups in Inverness. Unfortunately, the damage to the relationships between Donald and those leaving would never be repaired.

When I joined the Society there was a membership of approximately 30 members as I remember. These people varied in age from 10 years old to people in their 70's. There was a wide variety of styles and abilities within the Society, but all were asked to play with the same bowing and in the same military style. As they played all were watched meticulously by Donald and although never directly pointed at, were made aware somehow that all was not right if the bowing they were playing was incorrect.

Lessons at Clunes were always interesting. The croft house was in a degree of disrepair back then, quite cold in general as there was no double glazing and little insulation. The fire was always on as I remember and never gave out a vast amount of heat. The house was filled with fiddles, chanters, old photo's, shotguns, lots of cats and the occasional piglet. Geordie, Donald's youngest son had taken to pig farming on the croft and there would be regular attempts to assist piglets who had perhaps suffered from pneumonia and so they would be taken into the house and bathed.

A lesson cost £1 and would extend to anything between 1 and 2 hours......this would consist of Donald going through last weeks tune, amending any discrepancies, and threatening you with the same tune again. Revision of tunes was always on the agenda and was not appreciated by any pupil...it was always exciting to leave with a new tune to learn, never the one from the week before.

Donald at the gable end of his croft – cigarette invariably in his hand.

The £1 charged for each lesson would invariably be spent on cigarettes……there was always a gold packet of Benson and Hedges nearby and at the ready. A cigarette would be lit before Donald would proceed in writing out a new tune for you. More often than not the cigarette would not leave his mouth causing a full 2 inch length of ash to dangle precariously above the manuscript or indeed the fiddle if he decided he was going to demonstrate the tune for you.

As the years went by following this weekly routine he would spend a lot of time creating competitiveness between his pupils. He would extoll the virtues of one pupils playing to another and when there were competitions coming up he would use a great deal of psychology and adversarial tactics in getting you to practise. Competitions were a big part of learning under Donald and although I have never embraced them as part of my adult musical life, I very much see the benefit of them in a child's musical life. Competitions as a child gave you drive: The drive to practise and the drive to be a better player. He could see this and encouraged all his pupils to compete. By the time I was into my teens, I had won a lot of competitions at local and national level. I won the Junior Golden Fiddle Award which was sponsored by the Daily Record at the age of 13 which gave me the opportunity to perform solo at the Usher Hall in Edinburgh. Various National Mod competitions were won among other fiddle festivals across the country and all of this gave me the impetus to practise more and develop my playing. They were of great value to me over these early years.

I continued with Donald and our weekly lessons until I was around 16 years old. By this time we had progressed to the classic tunes of Neil Gow, Nathaniel Gow and William Marshall, as well as the more difficult tunes of Skinner, the Mathematician and the likes…

Around this time I arrived at Clunes for a lesson and out of the blue he told me that he would not want to teach me weekly any more. He said that he felt that he had taught me as much as he could. I was quite taken aback as this was a complete change of tack for him. He also followed this by saying that I was to no longer to play like Donald Riddell, I had to now learn to play like Duncan Chisholm. This was in effect him throwing me out of the nest. Everything that had been instilled in me from that early age was of course still there, especially the bowing technique, but I guess I had started to experiment playing with my own style to a certain extent and he probably saw that. He picked the right time and then made the decision to tell me. It was a moment I will never forget.

This sentence "I had to learn to play like Duncan Chisholm" is a short one but one that has spanned most of my professional life. In my later teenage years I would listen to Aly Bain, Johnny Cunningham and lots of Irish fiddle players. These players influenced me in terms of the tunes that they were playing rather than the style of fiddle music they played. I loved their overall sound and would listen to them rather than play like them. Throughout these early years I continued to have a Riddell influence in my playing but gradually as the years went by my own style emerged out of this and as I get older it continues to change organically as my views on music and the art of music change.

The Final Word by Duncan

My own musical journey has given me a very privileged life, a life that has taken me far from the croft at Clunes where I began my craft. My Journey has enabled me to express the way I feel about my own history, my family, and the landscape of my ancestral home with the Strathglass Trilogy. It has given me the canvas on which to draw imaginary pictures of Sandwood Bay. It has given me a world of friends and experiences that I could never have dreamed of as that captivated seven year old boy in the hall at Inchmore.

Music for me will always be cathartic, it will always make me feel better, it will make me whole. Music gives me the ability for self-expression and communication when sometimes words aren't enough. It lets me speak with people and tell them how I feel, how I think.

This gift has been passed down to me and to others through Donald Riddell from Alexander Grant. Although we are very different people, myself and Donald Riddell and in the same way Alexander Grant share something intangible.

In our lives we have shared and nurtured a musical thread that runs 1,000 years into the past. This thread of our tradition that has survived in spite of our Country's fraught history. It flourishes in the 21st century because of people such as Riddell and Alexander Grant, and God Willing will run 1,000 years into the future.

Alexander 'Battan' Grant

1856 - 1942

(His Life and Legacy)

Part 5 Afterword

Tonal and Vibrational Properties of Violins - and the Physics of Harmonic Wood.

The Violin

Man's greatest challenge to replicate the human voice with a bowed stringed instrument.

It would be something of a truism to say that Grant was fairly consumed by his desire to improve on the tonal qualities of the violins which he built. Hours and hours of dedicated effort must have gone into making and improving the tonal vibrational qualities of his violins. So much so, as presented earlier and in Figure 1, he developed his own concept for the body of the instrument which he called a 'Rondello'. Grant made around six of these, including work on a 'Roncello' - the sound box of one of these is held in the IMAG store room.

Figure 1 A Grant Rondello on Display at IMAG

He did not succeed in his efforts, but it could be said that he did not fail in making a type of instrument which has decided physical similarities to other bowed stringed instruments, such as the Chinese Huqin, Figure 2, of which there are a multitude of variants (roughly around 80 have been catagorised). These instruments have been around for much longer periods in history than Grant's, possibly even more so than the violin – so where did Grant get his idea from, or was it completely out of his own head?

Inverness always had its own harbour. Perhaps a sailor or shipping trader could have had the first type of disc-shaped violin or single-stringed instrument with something akin to a tin can or box shape at the bottom to amplyfy the sound. Had he seen one of these instruments before is a question which we cannot answer. [Was there a Chinese fore-runner to 'Sunny Jim' in Neil Munroe's classic 'The Vital Spark', siting on deck of an evening plonking away?]

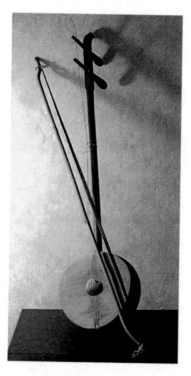

Figure 2 A Chinese Huqin

This, of course, is speculation, but surprisingly there is a great deal of speculation even in the modern world when it comes to analysing the tonal qualities of a violin, and why the great Cremonese masters of the craft could make such good instruments. It can be said without any speculation that Grant failed in his pursuit of perfection for a number of reasons, not least because the construction of a disc-shaped fiddle with seven internal sound posts was going to be very difficult to achieve, coupled with a lack of adequate sound projection. He had no recourse to scientific instruments which could aid his analysis of the harmonics of the instument, no heritage to fall back on in the making of violins which the great masters of the craft had built up over hundreds of years.

He did, however, succeed in making very good playable violins, if the opinions of the top fiddlers in the Highlands are anything to go by. Those who have played on the Grant violin in Morisons Ironmongers in Beauly have praised the tonal qualities of the instrument.

What Makes a Great Violin?

The violin is the most highly developed and most sophisticated of all stringed instruments. It emerged in Northern Italy about 1550, in a form that has remained essentially unchanged ever since. The famous Cremonese violin-making families of Amati, Stradivari and Guarneri formed a continuous line of succession that flourished from about 1600 to 1750, with skills being handed down from father to son and from master to apprentice.

Violins by the great Italian makers are, of course, beautiful works of art in their own right, and are coveted by collectors as well as players. Particularly outstanding ones have reputedly changed hands for over a million pounds. In contrast, fine modern instruments typically cost about £10,000, while factory-made violins for beginners can be bought for under £100. Do such prices really reflect such large differences in quality?

The Myths and Unknowns

Anecdote: During the course of producing this book, two or three violins with a Stradivarius label inside came up for auction at the Dingwall Auction Mart. As is well known, cows and sheep are the usual trading items, so an alert purchaser will most likely realise that this is a most unlikely place to find a Stradivarius violin at a cheap price.

When enquiring of a violin up for auction, the sale room assistant jokingly (I thought!) said it would be a Stradivari – he proceeded to his office and returned holding a magnifying glass. Low and behold there was the famous name printed in presumably authentic manner visible inside, on what looked like a label that had been stained with tea!

Never rely on the label inside the violin to spot a fake instrument as the label will probably have been forged as well.

It is interesting to note however, that Grant worked on (and 'improved') an instrument which he believed to be a Stradivari. This instrument is held at IMAG, awaiting the inspection of any historian of violins, see Part 1. However, the carving of the f-holes often helps to identify the maker of a valuable instrument.

Wood

Stradivarius violins are famous for their beautiful tone, and for years musicians, violin makers and scientists have wondered what makes these instruments so special. One theory is that it is at least in part due to the spruce wood used. The best violins are made from very hard, dense wood produced by slow-growing trees. By looking at the growth rings in the wood, scientists have found that, although the density of the wood used in modern and old violins is relatively similar, there is a big difference when comparing the early and late growth rings. The legendary Stradivarius violins have a much lower density difference than modern versions, which affects the vibrational efficiency and thus sound production. Scientists believe the unique density is due to the 'Little Ice Age' that hit Europe from the mid-1400s to the mid1800s, which meant cooler summers and longer winters. The trees that Antonio Stradivari used to make his violins between 1680 and 1720 would therefore have been even more slow growing than normal throughout their lifetime.

The wood – spruce for the top, willow for the internal blocks and linings, and maple for the back, ribs, and neck – grew during the Maunder Minimum, characterised by harsh winters and short summers that led to slower growth and more uniform annual rings. It is important to know that the speed of sound in wood increases with stiffness – the resistance of an elastic body to deformation by an applied force – of the material, and decreases with the density. All wood decay fungi reduce density, but the majority also reduce the speed of sound.

The Scientific Challenge

Modern science has now found that the application of the vegetative state of two fungi, Physisporinus vitreous for the top plate, and Xylaria for the bottom plate, which have thread-like cells will actively colonise the wood. These fungi secrete enzymes which can ultimately alter the wood structure and its acoustic properties. Once an optimum wood density loss has been induced in the top and bottom plates by the wood decay fungi, the wood can be sterilised with ethylene oxide, killing the bacteria and fungi. An important side effect of the fungal treatment is the reduction of the often irritating high notes of a violin, and makes the instrument sound warmer and mellower.

The consequence of this process is that wood density is reduced; damping is increased, while the modulus of elasticity remains unchanged. The method can improve the acoustic properties of resonance wood – particularly as it is becoming increasingly difficult to find superior resonance wood due to the impact of global warming.

Did Stradivarius have a secret?

Many theories have been put forward to claim that Stradivarius did have a secret method which he used in the construction of his violins. The most popular for well over a century has been that the varnish had some sort of 'magic' composition. The main function of the varnish is to protect the instrument from dirt and to stop it absorbing moisture from the players hands. This also imparts great aesthetic value to the instrument, with its translucent coating highlighting the beautiful grain structure of the wood below.

However, historical research has shown that the varnish is no different to that used by many furniture makers when Stradivari was alive. Researchers at Cambridge University, for example, have used electron microscopy to identify many of the important ingredients of the varnish itself, and the materials that are used to smooth the surface before the varnish is applied. It turns out that most could easily have been bought from the pharmacist shop next to Stradivari's workshop. Apart from the possibility that the varnish was contaminated with the wings of passing insects and debris from the workshop floor, there is no convincing evidence to support the idea of a secret formula!

Indeed, ultraviolet photography has revealed that many fine-sounding Italian violins have lost almost all their original varnish, and were recoated during the 19th century or later. The composition of the varnish is therefore unlikely to be the long-lost secret, although too much varnish would certainly increase the damping and therefore sully the tone.

Other researchers, meanwhile, have claimed that Stradivari's secret was to soak the wood in water, to leach out supposedly harmful chemicals, before it was seasoned. Although this would be consistent with the idea that the masts and oars of recently sunken Venetian war galleys might have been used to make violins, the scientific and historical evidence to support this view is unconvincing.

This raises the first point of contention – is there really a lost secret that sets Stradivarious violins apart from the best instruments made in Grant's time or indeed today? After more than a hundred years of vigorous debate, this question remains highly contentious, provoking strongly held but divergent views among playes, violin makers and scientists alike. All of the greatest violinists of modern times certainly believe it to be true, and invariably perform on violins by Stradivari or Guarneri in preference to modern instruments. The popular belief is that their unsurpassed skills, together with the magical 'Stradivarius secret', were lost by the start of the 19th century.

The choice of high-quality wood for making instruments has always been recognized by violin makers, and well-seasoned wood is generally recommended. However, by measuring the pattern of growth-rings in the wood of a Stradivarius, it is revealed that the Italian violin makers sometimes used planks of wood that had only been seasoned for five years. However, such wood is now 300 years old, and the intrinsic internal damping will almost certainly have decreased with time, as the internal organic structure has dried out.

The same will obviously be true for all old Italian instruments. The age of the wood may therefor automatically contribute to the improved quality of the older instruments. This may also explain why the quality of a modern instrument appears to change in its first few years. Surprisingly, many players still believe that their instruments improve because they are loved and played well, which would be very difficult to explain on any rational scientific basis!

Over the last 150 years, physicists have made considerable progress in understanding the way the violin works. In the 19th century the 'modernized' Stradivarius violin emerged with an 'enhanced' tone as a result of scientifically guided 'improvements' by the leading violin restorers of the day. However, Stradivari would be amazed to find that the modern musical world credits him with such a secret. After all, how could he possibly have had the clairvoyance to foresee that his instruments would be extensively modified in the 19th century to produce the kind of sound we value so highly today? Indeed, those sounds would have been totally alien to the musical tastes of his time.

Science has not provided any convincing evidence for the existence or otherwise of any measurable property that would set the Cremonese instruments apart from the finest violins made by skilled craftsmen today. Indeed, some leading soloists do occasionally play on modern instruments. However, the really top soloists, and, not surprisingly, violin dealers, who have a vested interest in maintaining the Cremonese legend of intrinsic superiority, remain unconvinced.

Quality and Excellence of Craftmanship

Every violin, whether a Stradivarius or the cheapest factory made copy, has a distinctive 'voice' of its own. Just as any musician can immediately recognise the difference between the voices of great Opera singers singing the same operatic aria, so a skilled violinist can distinguish between different qualities in the sound produced by individual Stradivari or Guarneri violins. The ability to do so represents a high challenge to express in scientific terms and to quantify (in numbers) how this is achieved. The challenge from a scientific point of view is to characterise such differences by physical measurements. Indeed, over the last century and a half, many famous physicists have been intrigued by the workings of the violin, with Helmholtz, Savart and Raman all making vital contributions.

However, it is important to recognize that the sound of the great Italian instruments we hear today is very different from the sound they would have made in Stradivari's time. Almost all Cremonese instruments underwent extensive restoration, and "improvement" in the 19th century. You need only listen to 'authentic' baroque groups, in which most top performers play on fine Italian instruments restored to their former state, to recognize the vast difference in tone quality between these restored originals and 'modern' versions of the Cremonese violins.

Prominent among the 19th century violin restorers was the French maker Vuillaume. Vuillaume worked closely with Felix Savart, best known to physicists for the Biot-Savart law in electromagnetism, to enhance the tone of early instruments. Vuillaume, Savart and others wanted to produce more powerful and brilliant sounding instruments that could stand out in the larger orchestras and concert halls of the day. Improvements in instrument design were also introduced to support the technical demands of great violin virtuosi such as Paganini.

Naturally - The Importance of Build Quality

So how do skilled violin makers optimize the tone of an instrument during the construction process? They begin by selecting a wood of the highest possible quality for the front and back plates, which they test by tapping with a hammer and judging how well it rings.

The next important step is to skilfully carve the plates out of the solid wood, taking great care to obtain the right degree of arching and variations in thickness. The craftsman has to learn how to adjust the plates to produce a fine-sounding instrument. Traditional makers optimise the thickness by testing the 'feel' of the plates when they are flexed, and by the sounds produced when they are tapped at different positions with the knuckles. This is the traditional equivalent of nodal analysis, with the violin maker's brain providing the interpretative computing power.

However, in the last 50 years or so, a group of violin makers has emerged who have tried to take a more overtly scientific approach to violin making. The pioneer in this field was Carleen Hutchins, the doyenne of violin acoustics in the US. She founded the Catgut Society of America in 1958, together with William Saunders of 'Russel-Saunders coupling' fame and John Schelling, a former director of radio research at Bell Labs. The society brings together violin makers and scientists from across the world, with the common aim of advancing our understanding of violin acoustics and developing scientific methods to help makers improve the quality of their instruments.

One common practice that has been adopted by violin makers has been to replace the traditional flexing and tapping of plates by controlled measurements. During the carving process, the thinned plates are suspended horizontally above a large loudspeaker. The acoustic resonances excited by it can readily be identified by sprinkling glitter onto the surface of the plates. When the loudspeaker has excited a resonance, the glitter bounces up and down, and moves towards the nodal lines of the resonant modes excited, much as in the same way that iron fillings, when placed above a bar magnet on a sheet of paper, will display the field lines of the magnet when tapped. The aim is to interactively thin or 'tune' the first few free-plate resonances to specified frequencies and nodal patterns.

Unfortunately, there are very few examples of such measurements for really fine Italian instruments because their owners are naturally reluctant to allow them to be taken apart for the sake of science. The relatively few tests that have been performed suggest that the early Italian makers may have tuned the resonant modes of the individual plates – which they could identify as they tapped them – to exact musical intervals. This would be consistent with the prevailing Renaissance view of 'perfection', which was measured in terms of numbers and exact ratios.

Members of the 'scientific' school of violin makers might reasonably claim that this could be the lost Stradivarius secret. However, it must indeed have been a secret, since there is no historical evidence to support the case. Although many first-class modern violins have been built based on these principles, there is little evidence to suggest that they are any better than many fine instruments made with more traditional methods.

However, neither traditional craftmanship nor scientific methods can hope to control the detailed resonant structure of an instrument in the acoustically important range above 1 kHz. Even the tiniest changes in the thickness of the plates will significantly affect the specific resonances in this frequency range. Furthermore, the frequencies and distribution of the resonant modes of the violin depend on the exact position of the sound post, which imposes an additional constraint on the modes that can be excited. Top players regularly return their instruments to violin makers, who move the sound post and adjust the bridge in an effort to optimize the sound. This means that there is no unique set of vibrational characteristics for any particular instrument – not even a Stradivarius!

As noted above, a key factor that affects the quality of a violin is the internal damping of the wood. This strongly affects the multi-resonant response of the instrument and the overall background at high frequencies. In particular, the difference between the peaks and troughs of the resonant response is determined by the quality-factor of the resonances. This largely depends on internal losses within the wood when it vibrates: only a small fraction of the energy is lost by acoustic radiation.

How Did the Great Masters Produce the Instruments Shape?

It goes without saying that the violin is a unique instrument in more ways than one – particularly with reference to its outline shape. How was it that the great masters came to design their instruments in such a uniform way with so little variation on the dimensions between makers? Over the centuries the shape has converged to what we are all familiar with today. The following method is described by Kerr based on work by Morgan and Reid.

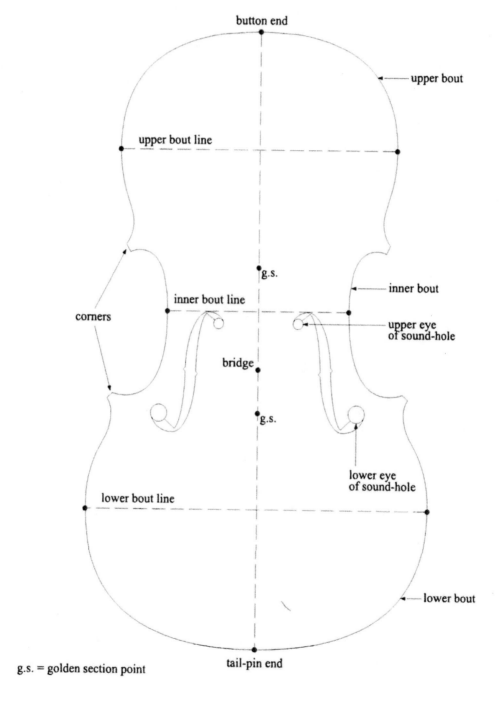

Figure 3 Principle Defining Features of a Violin

Surprisingly as it may seem, it appears that they were using the same rule as the master painters who preceded them used to create the division of geometric space on their canvas. Using modern equipment, these construction lines can now be made visible beneath the paint on some Leonardo works and several others. The technique was not a secret as such and would have been known by the Cremonese violin makers. This rule is termed the 'Golden Rule', in which the whole is equal to the sum of the lesser plus the greater part. A golden section can be created from a single dimension, e.g. say in this case the length you wish to make the body of the violin (AB). Locating C at its mid-point extend a line to cut a normal (90 degree) line AD. From C, CD describes an arc to intersect BA extended at E. A is the golden section point and divides BE in the golden ratio. The rule holds for any dimension and is always equal to 1.618…….181818 on and on. This is shown below.

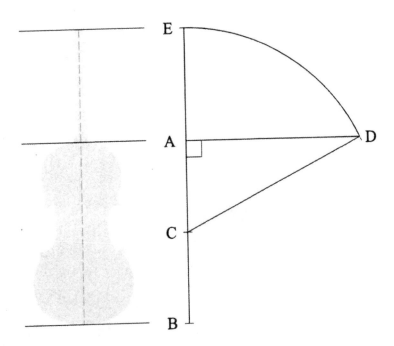

Figure 4 A Golden Ratio Constructed Using a Set of Dividers and a Straight Edge

Intriguingly even the fret spacing on a guitar uses the same method to position them on the finger board, as shown in Figure 5 below, where each successive interspace is 1.618 greater than the previous one. (the Golden ratio is in fact an irrational non-repeating number like pie).

Figure 5 Guitar Frets Spaced in Accordance with the Golden Rule

Hence it transpires that the great master violin makers did not need to resort to any clever mathematics to construct a plan shape for their instruments. They simply used straight lines and ratios of numbers to divide up the space and produce the outline of the instrument. This was quite an astonishing achievement done by using only a starting dimension, with no other numbers added, they could arrive at the defining shape we are all so familiar with as shown in Figures 3, 20 and 21, The method is explained diagrammatically as follows.

Firstly, it is a straight forward task to construct a curved line between any two points using a straight edge as shown below.

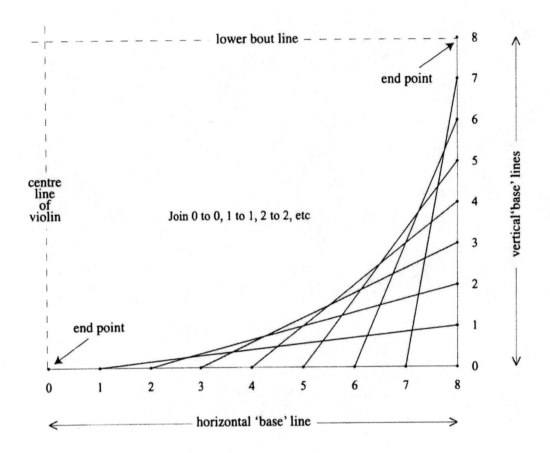

Figure 6 Generating a Curve from Straight Lines

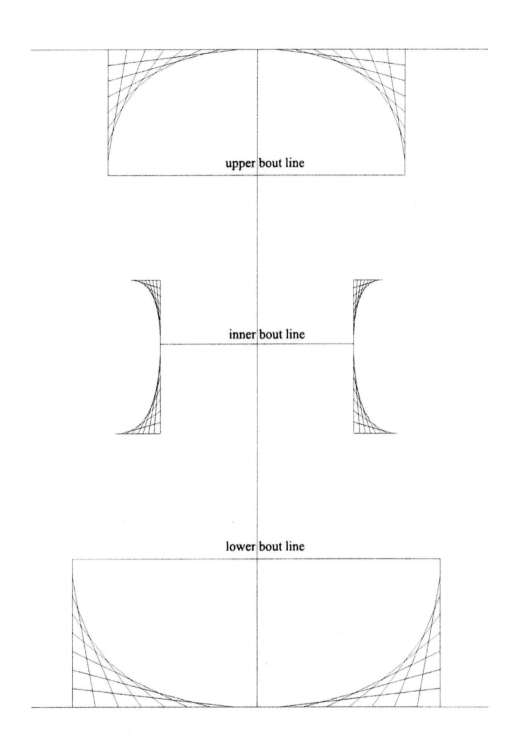

upper bout line

inner bout line

lower bout line

Figure 7 Curved Corners Created by the Method Shown Above

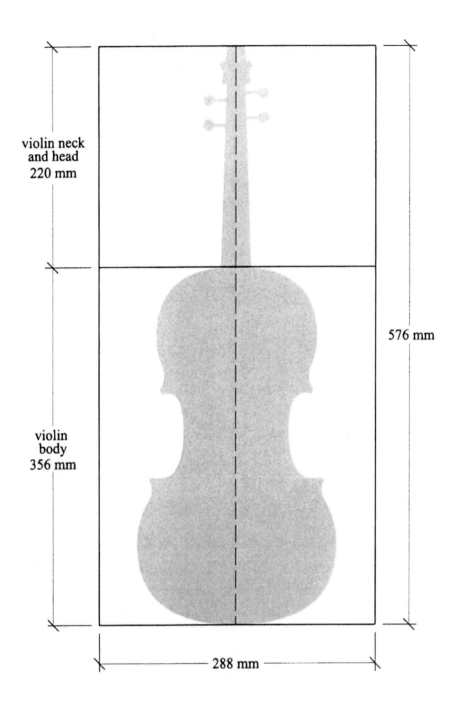

violin neck
and head
220 mm

576 mm

violin
body
356 mm

288 mm

Figure 8 Violin Frame Based on a 2:1 Rectangle

(356 mm, the chosen body length, is within a few mm of the body dimension of a Cremonese violin)

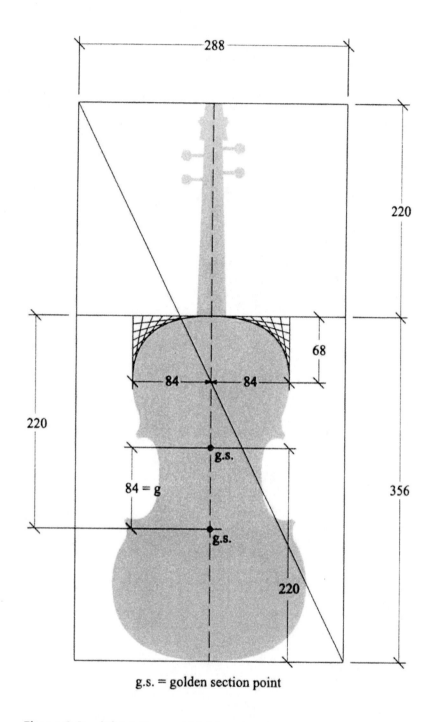

g.s. = golden section point

Figure 9 Straight Edge and Dividers Used to Position the Bouts

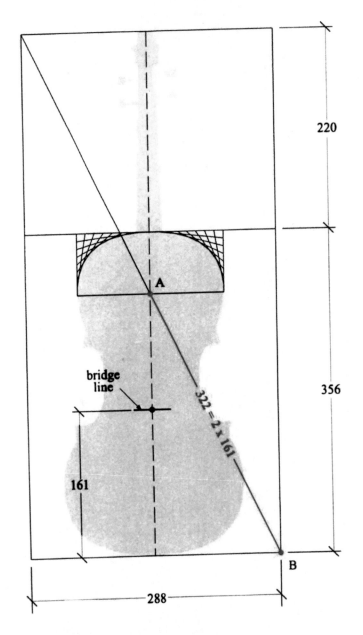

Figure 10 Derivation of the Bridge Line

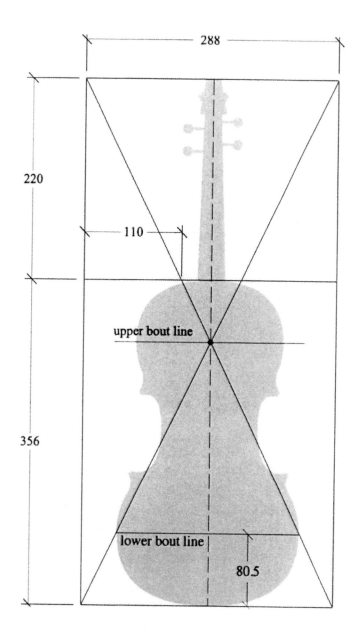

Figure 11 Position and Width of the Lower Bout

from the 2:1 Rectangle

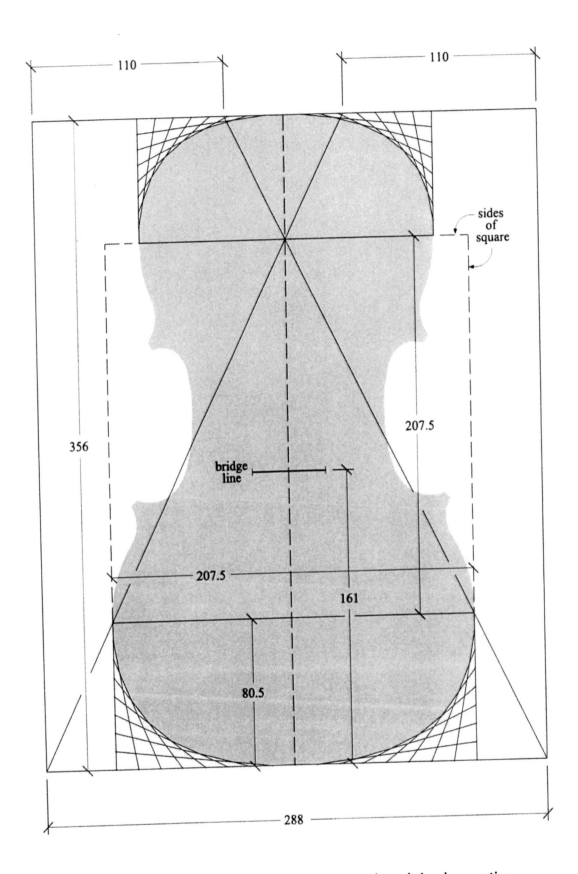

Figure 12 Position and width of the Lower Bout based simply on ratios

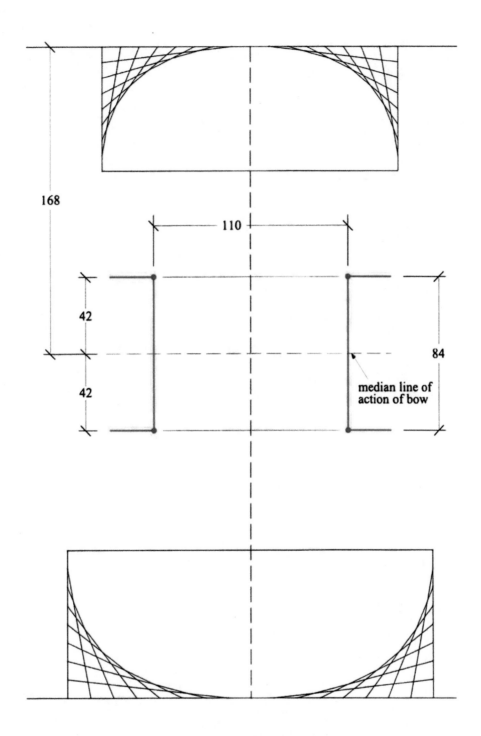

Figure 13 Locating the Inner Bouts

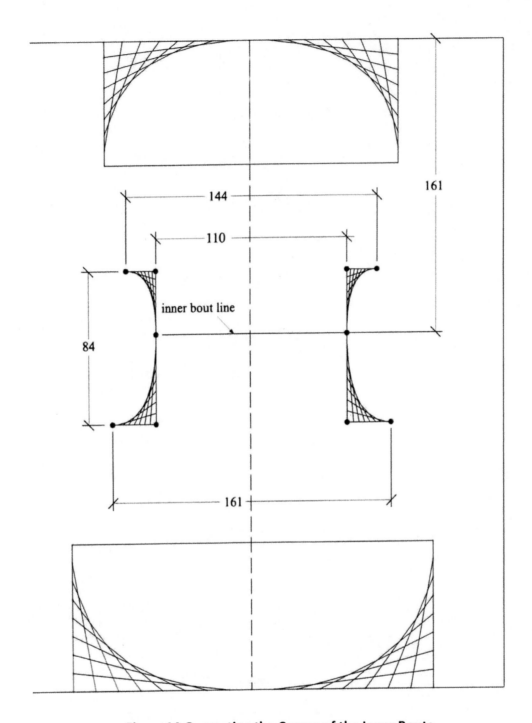

Figure 14 Generating the Curves of the Inner Bouts

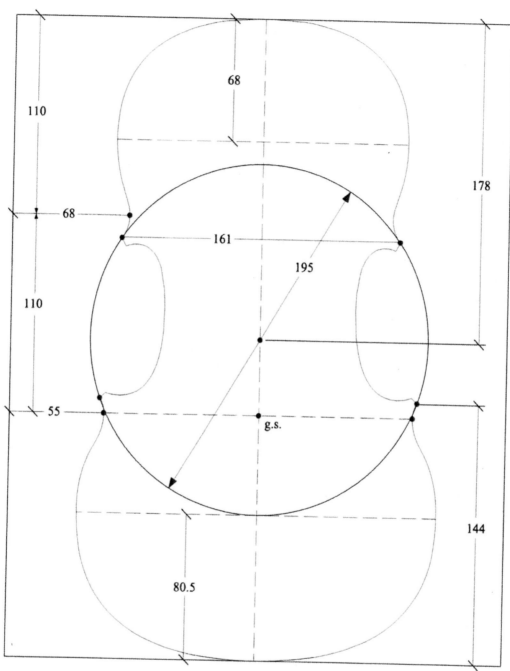

g.s. = golden section point

Figure 15 Locating the Corners

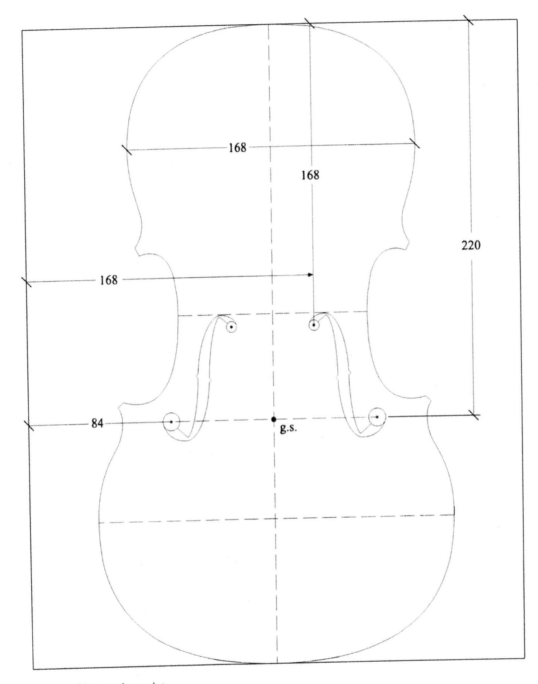

g.s. = golden section point

Figure 16 Locating the Eyes of the Sound Holes

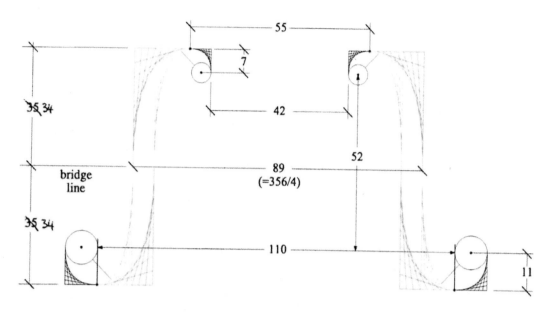

Figure 17 Curves of the Sound Holes

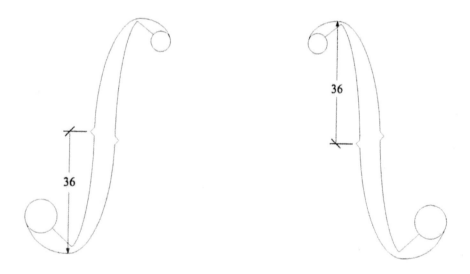

Figure 18 Locating the 'Nicks'

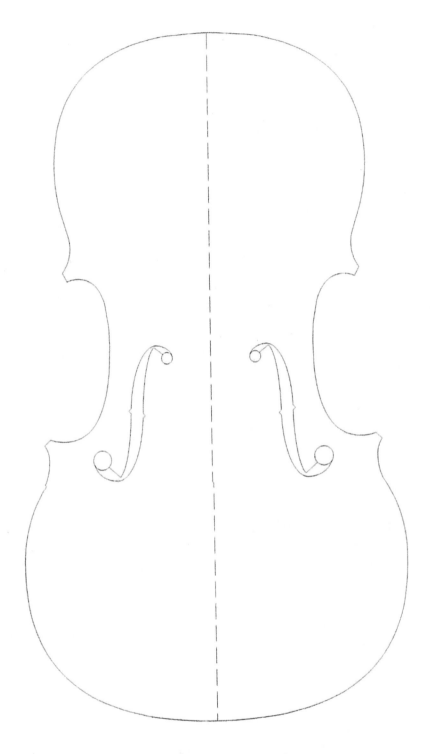

Figure 19 Finished Outline of the Violin

Figure 20 Comparison with the "Betts" Stradivari

Figure 21 Comparison with the "Alard" Stradivari

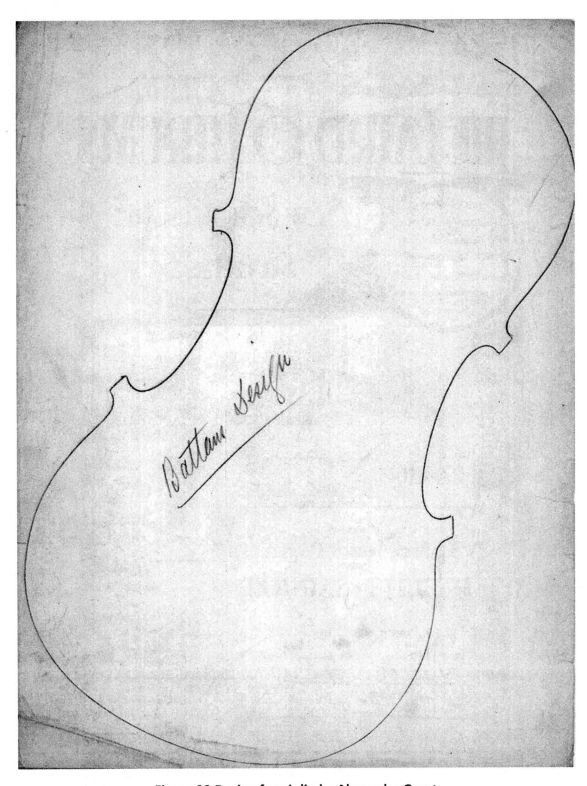

Figure 22 Design for violin by Alexander Grant.

This pencil outline of a fiddle body, named 'Battan Design', is drawn on the reverse of a piece of sheet music in the Grant collection. Grant would most definitely not have used the method just described. How close it resembles any of the instruments he made is a task still to be undertaken - if possible.

The Function of the Main Components of a Violin

The bridge piece and front and back plates are illustrated in Figure 23. Sound is produced by drawing a bow across one or more of the four stretched strings. The string tensions are adjusted by turning pegs at one end of the string, so that their fundamental frequencies are about 200, 300, 440 and 660 Hz – which corresponds to the notes G, D, A and E. However, the strings themselves produces almost no sound.

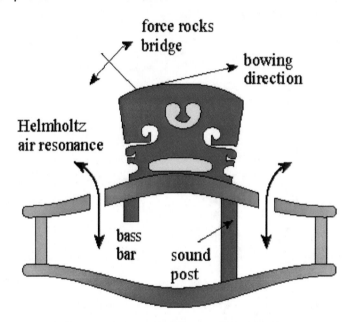

Figure 23 Essential parts of the violin

To produce sound, energy from the vibrating string is transferred to the main body of the instrument – the so-called sound box. The main plates of the violin act rather like a loudspeaker cone, and it is the vibration of these plates that produce most of the sound.

The strings are supported by the 'bridge', which defines the effective vibrating length of the string, and also acts as a mechanical transformer. The bridge converts the transverse forces of the strings into the vibrational modes of the sound box. Because the it has its own resonant modes, it plays a key role in the overall tone of the instrument. It is not entirely clear if Grant made his own bridge pieces as he preferred to buy in some parts - though the illustration shown in Figure 24, from the contents of his work shop, would indicate that he may have made his own.

The front plate is carved from a solid block of fine-grained pine. Maple is usually used for the back plate and pine for the sides. Two expertly carved and elegantly shaped 'f-holes' are also cut into the front plate as shown in Figure 25.

The f-holes play a number of important acoustic roles. By breaking up the area of the front plate, they affect its vibrational modes at the highest frequencies. More importantly, they boost the sound output at low frequencies. This occurs through the 'Helmholtz air resonance', in which air bounces backwards and forwards through the f-holes. The resonant frequency is determined by the area of the f-holes and the volume of the instrument. It is the only acoustic resonance of the instrument over which violin makers have almost complete control.

Figure 24 Bridge pieces held in the Grant collection

Early in the 16th century it was discovered that the output of stringed instruments could be increased by wedging a solid rod – the 'sound post' – between the back and front plates, close to the feet of the bridge. The force exerted by the bowed strings causes the bridge to rock about this position, causing the other side of the plate to vibrate with a larger amplitude. This increases the radiating volume of the violin and produces a much stronger sound.

The violin also has a 'bass bar' glued underneath the top plate, which stops energy being dissipated into acoustically inefficient higher-order modes. The bass bar and sound post were both made bigger in the 19th century to strengthen the instrument and to increase the sound output.

Figure 25 From the Grant collection

The Scientific Analysis of How Strings Vibrate

In the 19th century the German physicist Hermon von Helmholtz showed that when a violin string is bowed, it vibrates in a way that is completely different from the sinusoidal standing waves that are familiar to all physicists. Although the string vibrates back and forth parallel to the bowing direction, Helmholtz showed that other transverse vibrations of the string could also be excited, made up of straight-line sections. These are separated by 'kinks' that travel back and forth along the string and are reflected at the ends. The kinks move with the normal transverse-wave velocity, $c = (T/m)^{1/2}$, where T is the tension and m the mass per unit length of the string. The bowing action excites a Helmholtz mode with a single kink separating two straight sections, Figure 26.

When the kink is between the bow and the fingered end of the string, the string moves at the same speed and in the same direction as the bow. Only a small force is needed to lock the two modes together. This is known as the 'sticking regime' (Figure 26a). But as soon as the kink moves past the bow, on its way to the bridge and back, the string slips past the bow and starts moving in the opposite direction to it. This is known as the 'slipping' regime' (Figure 26b).

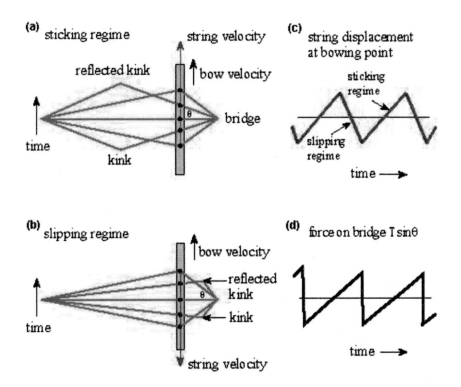

Figure 26 Dynamics of the Bow and Strings

Although the sliding friction is relatively small in the slipping regime, energy is continuously transferred from the strings to the vibrational modes of the instrument at the bridge. Each time the kink reflects back from the bridge and passes underneath the bow, the bow has to replace the lost energy. It therefore exerts a short impulse on the string so that it moves again at the same velocity as the bow.

This process is known as the 'slip-stick' mechanism of string excitation and relies on the fact that sliding friction is much smaller than sticking friction (Figure 26c). The Helmholtz wave generates a transverse force $T\sin\theta$ on the bridge, where θ is the angle of the string at the bridge. This force increases linearly with time, but its amplitude reverses suddenly each time the kink is reflected at the bridge, producing a sawtooth waveform (Figure 26d). The detailed physics of the way the bow excites a string has been extensively studied by J. McIntyre and J. Woodhouse at Cambridge University, who have made a number of important theoretical and experimental contributions to violin acoustics in recent years.

It is important to recognise that the Helmholtz wave is a free mode of vibration of the string. The player has to apply just the right amount of pressure to excite and maintain the waveform without destroying it. The lack of such skill is one of the main reasons why the sound produced by a beginner is so excruciating. Conversely, the intensity, quality and subtlety of sound produced by great violinists is mainly due to the fact that they can control the Helmholtz waveform with the bow. The quality of sound produced by any violin therefore depends as much on the bowing skill of the violinist as on the physical construction of the instrument. One of the reasons that the great Cremonese violins sound so wonderful is because we hear them played by the world's greatest players.

The Transformation of String Vibrations to Sound

The sawtooth force that is generated on the top of the bridge by a bowed string is the input signal that forces the violin to vibrate and radiate sound (Figure 27) – rather like the electrical input to a loudspeaker, albeit with a much more complicated frequency response. The input sawtooth waveform has a rich harmonic content, consisting of numerous Fourier components. (Jean-Baptste Joseph Fourier – was a French mathematician who devised a mathematical proof, which showed that any waveform can be de-composed into a summation of all the individual sinusoidal waveform harmonics contained in the waveshape).

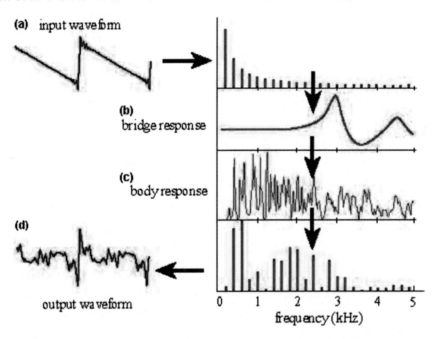

Figure 27 From Bowed Sawtooth Input at the Bridge to Melodic Output

Since the violin is a linear system, the same Fourier components or 'partials' (or overtones as Grant described them), appear in the output of the violin. The amplitude of each partial in the radiated sound is determined by the response of the instrument at that particular frequency. This is largely determined by the mechanical resonances of the bridge and by the body of the instrument. These resonances are illustrated schematically in Figure 26, where typical responses have been mathematically modelled to simulate their influence on the sound produced.

The Importance of the Bridge and the Transfer of Vibrations

At low frequencies, the bridge simply acts as a mechanical lever, since the response is independent of frequency. However, between 2.5 and 3 kHz the bowing action excites a strong resonance in the bridge, with the top rocking about its narrowed waist section. This boosts the intensity of any partials in this frequency range, where the ear is most sensitive, and gives greater brightness and carrying power to the sound. Another resonance occurs at about 4.5 kHz in which the bridge bounces up and down on its two feet. Between these two resonances there is a strong dip in the transfer of force to the body. Thankfully this dip decreases the amplitude of the partials at these frequencies, which the ear associates with an unpleasant shrillness in musical quality.

The sinusoidal force exerted by the bridge on the top plate produces an acoustic output that can be modelled mathematically. The output increases dramatically whenever the exciting frequency coincides with one of the many vibrational modes of the instrument. Indeed, the violin is rather like a loudspeaker with a highly non-uniform frequency response that peaks every time a resonance is excited. The modelled response is very similar to many recorded examples made on real instruments.

In practice, quite small changes in the arching, thickness and mass of the individual plates can result in big changes in the resonant frequencies of the violin, which is why no two instruments ever sound exactly alike. The multi-resonant response leads to dramatic variations in the amplitudes of individual partials for any note played on the violin.

Such factors must have unconsciously guided the radical redesign of the bridge in the 19th century. Violinists often place an additional mass (the 'mute') on top of the bridge, effectively lowering the frequency of the bridge resonances. This results in a much quieter and 'warmer' sound that players often use as a special effect. It is therefore surprising that so few players – or even violin makers – recognise the major importance of the bridge in determining the overall tone quality of an instrument. (Given the variety and number of different bridge pieces found in Grant's workshop archive, Figure 24, then perhaps he did).

One of the reasons for the excellent tone of the very best violins is the attention that top players give to the violin set-up – rather like the way in which a car engine is tuned to obtain the best performance. Violinists will, for example, carefully adjust the bridge to suit a particular instrument, or even select a different bridge altogether. The sound quality of many modern violins could undoubtedly be improved by taking just as much care in selecting and adjusting the bridge.

The transfer of energy from the vibrating string to the acoustically radiating structural modes is clearly essential for the instrument to produce any sound. However, this coupling must not be too strong, otherwise the instrument becomes difficult to play and the violinist has to work hard to maintain the Helmholtz wave. Indeed, a complete breakdown can occur when a string resonance coincides with a particularly strongly coupled and lightly damped structural resonance.

When this happens, the sound suddenly changes from a smooth tone to a quasi-periodic, uncontrollable, grunting sound – the 'wolf-note'. Players minimise this problem by wedging a duster against the top plate to dampen the vibrational modes, or by placing a resonating mass, the 'wolf-note adjuster', on one of the strings on the far side of the bridge. However, this only moves the wolf-note to a note that is not played as often, rather than eliminating it entirely.

The Helmholtz motion of the string and the wolf-note problem were extensively studied by the Indian physicist Chandrasekhara Raman in the early years of the 20th century. His results were published in a series of elegant theoretical and experimental papers soon after he founded the Indian Academy of Sciences and before the work on optics that earned him the Nobel Prize for Physics in 1930.

Tonal Quality, Resonances, and Instrument Design

The existence of so many resonances at almost random frequencies means that there is simply no such thing as a 'typical' waveform or spectrum for the sound from a violin. Indeed, there is just as much variation between the individual notes on a single instrument as there is between the same note played on different instruments. This implies that the perceived tone of a violin must be related to the overall design of the instrument, rather than to the frequencies of particular resonances on an instrument.

Is measured response a reliable guide to quality? Does it Help

An interesting attempt to look for such global properties was made at the turn of the century by the violin maker Heinrich Dunnwald in Germany. He measured the acoustic output of 10 Italian violins, 10 fine modern copies and 10 factory-made violins, all of which were excited by an electromagnetic driver on one side of the bridge (Figure 28). Between 400 and 600 Hz, the factory-made violins were found – surprisingly – to be closer to the Italian instruments than the modern copies. At frequencies above 1,000 Hz, however, the factory-made instruments had a rather weak response, in contrast to the over-strong response of the modern violins, which may contribute to a certain shrillness in their quality.

In practice it is extremely difficult to distinguish between a particularly fine Stradivarius instrument and an indifferent modern copy on the basis of the measured response alone. The ear is a supreme detection device and the brain is a far more sophisticated analyser of complex sounds than any system yet developed to assess musical quality.

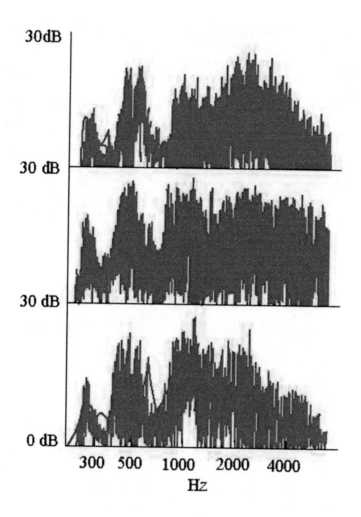

Figure 28 Typical acoustic output response of each of the three

different types of instruments tested

(Italian, fine modern copies, and factory made)

Although such measurements give the frequencies of important acoustic resonances, they tell us nothing about the way a violin actually vibrates. A powerful technique for investigating such vibrations is called "time-averaged interference holography". Bernard Richardson, a physicist at Cardiff University in the UK, has made a number of such studies on the guitar and violin. Some particularly beautiful examples for the guitar are shown in Figure 9. Unfortunately, it is not easy to obtain similar high-quality images for the violin because it is smaller, the vibrations of the surface are smaller, and the surfaces of the violin are more curved and less reflective than those of the guitar.

Another powerful approach is modal analysis: A violin is lightly struck with a calibrated hammer at several positions and the transient response at various points is measured with a very light accelerometer. These responses are then analysed by computer to give the resonant frequencies and structural modes of vibration of the whole instrument. This technique has been used to teach students about violin acoustics at the famous Mittenwald School of Violin Making in Germany and by Ken Marshall in the US. Marshall has also shown that the way the violin is held has little effect on its resonant response.

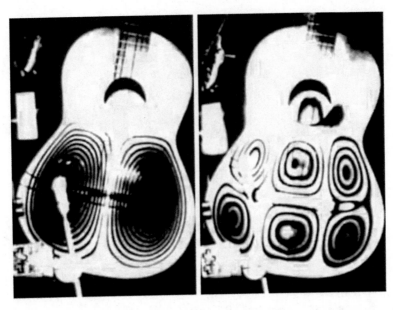

Figure 29 Interference Holography Pattern Illustrating Resonant

Vibrations Produced by a Guitar

Similar information can be obtained by finite-element analysis: the violin is modelled as a set of masses that are connected by springs, which makes it relatively straightforward to evaluate the resonant modes and associated vibrations of the whole structure. Various physical parameters of the materials used to make the violin can also be incorporated in the calculations. It is then possible to construct a virtual violin and to predict all its vibrational and acoustic properties. This might be the first step towards designing a violin with a specified response and hence tonal quality – once we know how to define 'quality' in a measurable way.

Is the use of vibrato an essential technical technique?

The strongly peaked frequency response of the violin has a dramatic influence on the sound produced when 'vibrato' is used. In this playing technique, the finger stopping the string is cyclically rocked backwards and forwards, periodically changing the pitch of the note. Because the response has such strong peaks and troughs, any change in pitch also produces cyclic variations in the overall amplitude, waveform and spectral content of the sound (Figure. 10).

The use of vibrato is very common nowadays because it captures and holds the attention of the listener, enabling the solo violin to be heard even when accompanied by a large orchestra. It would have been considered far less important when Stradivari was alive because vibrato was used only for special theatrical effects and the violin was expected to blend in with other instruments. Vibrato adds a certain 'lustre' and interest to the quality of sound produced because the ear is particularly sensitive to changes in the waveform. This in turn can result in the players subjective assessment of the sound as bringing 'life and vibrancy' to the sound.

To achieve such large changes in the frequency response of the violin, the individual resonances of the instrument have to be strongly peaked, which requires high-quality wood with low internal damping. Unfortunately, wood can absorb water, which increases the damping: This explains why violinists often notice that the responsiveness of an instrument, which includes the ability to control the sound quality using vibrato, changes with temperature and humidity.

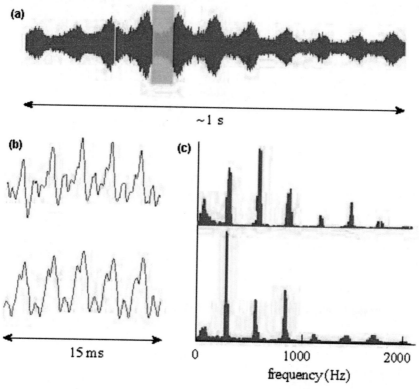

Figure 30 Strongly Peaked Resonances Result in Good Vibrato

Conclusion

Maybe there is an essential aspect of violin quality that we are still failing to recognise. Many violinists say they can distinguish an instrument with a fine 'Italian Cremonese sound' from one with, say, a more 'French' tone, such as a Vuillaume violin. But we still do not know how to characterize such properties in meaningful physical terms.

References:

1. McIntyre, M. E. and Woodhouse, J., :'On the Fundamentals of Bowed String Dynamics'. 1981, Acustica, 42 93.
2. Kerr, M. F., :'An account of violin Geometry'. Private Publication.
3. Gough, G., :'Science and the Stradivarius'. Pub. Physics World, 01 Apr. 2000'.
4. Fletcher, N. and H., Rossing, T. D., :'The Physics of Musical Instruments'. 2nd Edn., Springer, New York.
5. Hutchins, C. M. and Benade, V., :'Research Papers in Violin Acoustics'. 197593, vols 1 and 2, 1997. The Acoustical Society of America, New York.
6. Cremer, L., :'The Physics of the Violin'. MIT Press, (essential physics of violin acoustics).

General References:

Inverness Museum & Art Gallery (IMAG)

Highlife Highland Archive Services, Inverness (www.ambaile.org.uk)

Physics World, Published by the Institute of Physics

'A data-driven approach to violin making'. Scientific reports. Open Access.

Inverness Remembered, Inverness Courier, Vol.1V, Printed by Inverness Courier

'March Past - A Memoir by Lord Lovat'; Pub. By Weidenfeld & Nicolson

'The Story of the Lovat Scouts'; Michael Leslie Melville; Pub. By Strident Publishing Ltd

'Lord Lovat', *A Biography*. By the Rt. Hon. Sir Francis Lindley. Pub.By Hutchinson & Co

Scottish National Portrait Gallery

The Clunes Collection of Fiddle Music, Pub. By; Mrs J.F. Riddell & Mrs. R. Spankie

Memories of Beauly & Kilmorack, Facebook Page, Photo Archive

Acknowledgements:

Michael Kerr, Great Grandson of Alexander 'Battan' Grant

Donald Fraser at Donald Morison Ironmonger, Station Road, Beauly

Duncan Chisholm and Bruce MacGregor

Lord Lovat (16th), Clan Fraser

Drusilla Fraser – Photographs relating to (15th) Lord Lovat and family

Ian Marr, Marr Antiques, The Square, Beauly – for information relating to Donald Riddell

Cathleen MacDonald – for information relating to Donald Riddell

Scottish Television Film Archive, Donald Riddell with guests – Alison Wilkie

Robbie Shepherd interviews Donald Riddell Radio Scotland, 06/10/84

Quest for the Round Fiddle of Strathspey, Archie Fisher, Radio Scotland, 18/12/1976

Inverness Local History Forum– promotion of Lecture on Grant, (S. Gair)

Inverness Townscape Heritage Project – promotion of Lecture on Grant, (S. Gair)

General - Further Reading:

'Old Inverness in Pictures', Inverness Field Club; Paul Harris Publishing, 1978

'The Banks of the Ness', Mairi A MacDonald; Paul Harris Publishing, 1982

'The Last Highlander', Sara Fraser; Pub. Harper Press, 2012

'Past Forgetting', Veronica Fraser; Pub. REVIEW, 2002

'Memoirs of the Life of Simon Fraser Lord Lovat'; *A Reprint from the rare 1767 Edition, giving his Genealogy from Sir Simon Fraser the Patriot;* Pub. P. Fraser, Bookseller and Stationer, Beauly.

'The Gaelic Place Names and Heritage of Inverness', Roddy MacLean; Culcabock Publishing, Inverness, 2004

'Memoirs of William Collie', Sands and McDougall, limited, Printer, Melbourne, Australia, 1908. (A 19th Century Deerstalker).